Democracy, Elections and Good Governance in India

NIPA® GENX ELECTRONIC RESOURCES & SOLUTIONS P. LTD.
New Delhi-110 034

About the Authors

Dr. Rede G.D., An accomplished Agricultural Economist, currently serves as an Assistant Professor at Symbiosis Institute of Business Management, Nagpur, constituent of Symbiosis International (Deemed) University, Pune, Maharashtra, India. His academic credentials include a Ph.D. in Agricultural Economics from Bidhan Chandra Krishi Viswavidyalaya, Mohanpur, Nadia, West Bengal, alongside an M.Sc. in Agricultural Economics from Dr. Panjabrao Deshmukh Krishi Vidyapeeth, Akola, and a B.Sc. in Agriculture from Dr. Balasaheb Sawant Konkan Krishi Vidyapeeth, Dapoli, Maharashtra. Dr. Rede's commitment to excellence is underscored by his successful clearance of the ICAR JRF in Social Science and ICAR ASRB NET in Agricultural Economics. With six years of academic experience, Dr. Rede actively engages in teaching various U.G. courses of Agricultural Economics. His scholarly contributions extend beyond the classroom, with over thirty research papers published in reputable national and international journals, alongside authoring a book and four book chapters in esteemed publications. Dr. Rede demonstrates exceptional proficiency and unwavering dedication in both teaching and research. Recognized for his contributions, Dr. Rede has been honored with the Best Young Researcher and Young Scientist Award. He regularly participates and presents his research findings at National and International Conferences, Seminars, and Workshops across India. Additionally, Dr. Rede is a life member of several professional societies in the field of Agriculture and allied sciences, affirming his dedication to advancing knowledge and expertise in his domain.

Dr. Rohit S. Shelar, Is a highly accomplished scholar with a passion for research in Agriculture Extension. He obtained his graduate and post-graduate degrees from Dr. B.S. Konkan Krishi Vidyapeeth, Dapoli (MH). Continuing his pursuit of knowledge, he earned a doctoral degree from Banaras Hindu University, Varanasi with the prestigious ICAR-SRF fellowship. With a deep understanding of his field, he cleared the UGC NET with JRF and the ICAR NET in Agricultural Extension, showcasing his expertise. He has over three years of experience in teaching and research, leaving a lasting impact on students and fellow researchers. As an author, Dr. Rohit has contributed to more than fifteen research publications, gaining recognition for his innovative ideas and valuable insights. He actively participates in national and international conferences, collaborating with scholars and sharing his findings. Dr. Rohit also a life member of Indian Society of Extension Education, New Delhi and Society of Extension Education, Agra.

Dr. Jyoti Chaudhary (Assistant Professor, Agricultural Economics) born in Kangra District of Himachal Pradesh. She has completed B.Sc. Agriculture (2011-15) and M.Sc. (Agricultural Economics) from CSK Himachal Pradesh Krishi Vishwavidyalaya, Palampur. She is B.Sc. Agriculture Gold medalist. She is a life member of Indian Society of Agricultural Economics, Agricultural Economics Research Association and Indian Society of Tree Scientists. She joined the Department of Agricultural Economics Institute of Agricultural Sciences, Banaras Hindu University, Varanasi to pursue her Ph.D. in Agricultural Economics. At present she is working as an Assistant Professor, Department of Social Sciences, College of Horticulture and Forestry, Thunag Mandi, Dr YS Parmar University of Horticulture and Forestry, Nauni, Solan, Himachal Pradesh. She has participated and presented papers in number of national and international conferences, seminar and science congress on agricultural economics and agricultural subjects during 2015-2022. She has published various research papers, book chapter, popular articles and abstracts.

Dr. Saurav Singla is an expert in Agricultural Statistics and data analysis. After obtaining his graduation from Lovely Professional University, Jalandhar he went forward for pursuing Master's degree in Agricultural Statistics from Tamil Nadu Agricultural University, Coimbatore through ICAR JRF. He has done some remarkable work in the field of Artificial Intelligence and Machine Learning during his doctoral research while being at Banaras Hindu University, Varanasi. He was awarded with ICAR Seniors Research Fellowship during doctoral period. Further his expertise with statistics and data analysis earned him good name in the field and as a result he had done a lot of collaborative work with scientists of diverse fields. Dr. Singla has taught masters and PhD students several courses in the field of Statistics at Lovely Professional University after the completion of doctoral degree. He has guided two master's students for project and authored several research papers and book chapters in journals of good repute. Currently he is working as an Assistant Professor (Agril Statistics) at Sri Karan Narendra Agricultural University, Jobner, Rajasthan.

Democracy, Elections and Good Governance in India

Rede G.D.
Assistant Professor
Symbiosis Institute of Business Management
Nagpur, Maharashtra, India

Rohit S. Shelar
Assistant Professor
KR Marathe College of Agriculture
Phondaghat, Maharashtra, India

Jyoti Chaudhary
Assistant Professor
Department of Social Sciences
College of Horticulture and Forestry
Thunag Mandi, Himachal Pradesh, India

Saurav Singla
Assistant Professor (Agril Statistics)
Sri Karan Narendra Agricultural University
Jobner, Rajasthan, India

NIPA® GENX ELECTRONIC RESOURCES & SOLUTIONS P. LTD.
New Delhi-110 034

NIPA® GENX ELECTRONIC RESOURCES & SOLUTIONS P. LTD.

101,103, Vikas Surya Plaza, CU Block
L.S.C.Market, Pitam Pura, New Delhi-110 034
Ph : +91 11 27341616, 27341717, 27341718
E-mail: newindiapublishingagency@gmail.com
www: www.nipabooks.com

For customer assistance, please contact
Phone: + 91-11-27 34 17 17
Fax: + 91-11-27 34 16 16

ISBN: 978-93-58874-75-4

Composed and Designed by NIPA®.

Preface

In this book imperative concepts of democracy, decentralization with respect to good governance have been explicated clearly with sufficient examples from the concerned area. This book intend to provide evidence of democracy at grass root level, their relevant elections and about good governance for people's participation. Election commission in India, Local self-Government bodies, National level, State level, Munciple Cooperation and council, Nagar Panchayat, Zilla Parishad, Panchayat Samiti, Gram Panchayat and Constitutional provision of 73rd and 74th constitutional Amendment Act and their important features. The book also provides details about Nature of Good Governance with esteem of India, Attributes of Poor Governance and Steps taken for the establishment of Good Governance.

The whole material is presented in simple language for easy understanding. It will outfit the course as a text book for undergraduates in Agricultural Universities, Rural Universities and Traditional Universities. It also supports as reference book for student's teachers and admistrators who works at grass root level. The authors with a thoughtful thankfulness and esteems acknowledge their obligation to authors of various books, journals, periodicals, reports and bulletins from which they have comprehended the subject matter of book.

Contents

1

Democracy Meaning and Its Classification

Democracy is a system of government in which power is held by the people, either directly or through elected representatives. It is a form of government that allows for the free and fair participation of citizens in the decision-making process of the country. In a democratic system, all citizens have the right to vote and participate in the political process, and the government is accountable to the people. Key features of democracy include a free press, an independent judiciary, and the protection of individual rights and freedoms. While there are many variations of democracy, the basic principles include equality, freedom, and the rule of law.

Democracy is not a novel concept; rather, it has a long history. However, its embodiment philosophies and justification grounds have been revised from time to time. The term 'democracy' is difficult to define because it is ambiguous, as are other political terms such as liberty, equality, power, and so on. It is so because its perspective varies from person to person. In other words, what one person considers a model, another rejects. As a result, people have both positive and negative perceptions of democracy, and they argue accordingly. As a result, different minds interpret democracy differently.

Gandhi, one of the greatest thinkers of political thought, has elaborated on how democracy and nonviolence are inextricably linked and that one is dependent on the other for proper operation. He believed that true democracy is founded on nonviolence, and that the establishment of peace and the fulfilment of democracy are inextricably linked. As a result, he believed that "*ahimsa comes before swaraj.*" Democracy and violence cannot be reconciled and cannot coexist because a state whose means are tainted with violence, whether physical or non-physical, always results in a non-democratic state or a totalitarian regime. True democracy or the Swaraj of the masses can never be achieved through untruthful and violent means, for the simple reason that the natural corollary to their use would be the suppression or extermination of the antagonists. That does not imply individual liberty. Individual freedom can only be exercised fully under a regime of unadulterated ahimsa.

Abraham Lincoln is widely regarded as one of the greatest champions of democracy in American history. He believed in the idea of *government of the people, by the people, and for the people.* He saw democracy as a way to promote equality and ensure that everyone had a say in how the country was run. Lincoln believed that democracy required a commitment to individual rights and the rule of law.

Lincoln was also a strong believer in the idea of popular sovereignty, which held that the people should have the power to decide important political issues. He believed that this was essential for maintaining a functioning democracy and for ensuring that the government remained accountable to the people.

Concept of Democracy

The concept of democracy originated in ancient Greece, particularly in the city-state of Athens, where it was implemented in the form of a direct democracy. In this system, all citizens had an equal say in government decisions through participation in the assembly. Over time, the concept of democracy has evolved, and today, it can take many forms, including representative democracy, where citizens elect representatives to make decisions on their behalf, and liberal democracy, which incorporates the protection of individual rights and freedoms into the democratic system. In the modern world, democracy has developed from the American and French revolutions.

The word "democracy" comes from the Greek words "*demos*," meaning "people," and "*kratos*," meaning "rule" or "power." Therefore, the literal meaning of democracy is "rule of the people" or "power of the people." The term "democracy" has been used to describe various systems of government throughout history, but it continues to be associated with the idea of popular sovereignty and the rule of law.

A political system can properly be called democratic only if the government in power can be peacefully removed by a majority decision of the people, through fair and open elections. There are few nation states today that do not claim to be democratic, but not all would qualify on the basis of this criterion. The Universal Declaration of Human Rights, which was adopted and proclaimed by General Assembly resolution 217 A (III) of 10 December 1948, expressed the values of democracy in proclaiming that "the will of the people shall be the basis of the authority of government" (article 21) and considered it essential that "human rights should be protected by the rule of law" (Preamble).Not long afterwards, the General Assembly adopted its first explicit resolution on "Promoting and Consolidating Democracy".

a) Promoting pluralism.
b) Promoting, protecting and respecting all human rights.
c) Strengthening the rule of law.
d) Developing, nurturing and maintaining an electoral system that provides for the free and fair expression of the people's will through genuine and periodic elections.
e) Creating and improving the legal framework and necessary mechanisms for enabling the participation of all members of civil society in the promotion and consolidation of democracy.
f) Strengthening democracy through good governance.
g) Strengthening democracy by promoting sustainable development.
h) Enhancing social cohesion and solidarity.

Definitions

1. *"Democracy is the government of the people, by the people, for the people."* ***- Abraham Lincoln***

   This famous definition by Abraham Lincoln highlights the core principles of democracy, emphasizing the idea that power and governance should derive from the people themselves.

2. *"Democracy is a system that guarantees political freedom, protects minority rights, upholds the rule of law, and ensures accountability and transparency in governance."* ***- Amartya Sen***

   Amartya Sen, a Nobel laureate economist, highlights the essential elements of democracy, including political freedom, rights protection, rule of law, and good governance.

3. *"Democracy is not just a form of government; it is a way of life."*

   - Jawaharlal Nehru

   Jawaharlal Nehru, the first Prime Minister of India, emphasized that democracy is not merely a political system but a broader philosophy that encompasses principles of freedom, equality, and social progress.

Types of Democracy

There are several types of democracy, including:

1. **Direct democracy**: In this system, citizens participate directly in decision-making processes rather than through representatives. It is mostly suitable for smaller communities where people can easily gather and deliberate on issues affecting them.

Example: In Athens, all male citizens over the age of 18 could attend the Assembly, which was held several times a month on a hillside outside the city. At the Assembly, citizens could propose, debate, and vote on laws and other important issues.

Another example of direct democracy is Switzerland, where citizens can propose changes to the constitution or laws through popular initiatives, and can also vote on referendums to approve or reject laws passed by the parliament. This system of direct democracy allows citizens to have a direct say in the decisions that affect their lives.

2. **Representative democracy:** In this system, citizens elect representatives to make decisions on their behalf. The representatives are accountable to the people through periodic elections.

   An example of a representative democracy is the countries like India, United States of America. *etc.* In this system, citizens elect representatives to make decisions on their behalf. The citizens vote in elections for the President, members of parties, and state and local officials. These elected officials then make decisions and create laws based on the interests of their constituents. The citizens have the ability to hold their representatives accountable through voting and other forms of political participation. Other examples of representative democracies include the United Kingdom, Canada, and Australia.

3. **Presidential democracy:** This system features a separation of powers between the executive and legislative branches of government. The president is elected by the people and serves as both the head of state and head of government.

   For example, in the United States of America, the President serves as both the head of state and the head of government, with significant executive powers, including the power to veto legislation and command the military. The President is directly elected by the citizens through an electoral college system, separate from the election of members of Congress. The President serves for a fixed term and can be impeached by Congress for high crimes and misdemeanors. Other examples of presidential democracies include Brazil, Mexico, and France.

4. **Parliamentary democracy:** In this system, the executive branch is accountable to the legislature, which is composed of elected representatives. The head of government is usually the leader of the party or coalition that holds the majority in the legislature.

   An example of a parliamentary democracy is the India. In this system, citizens elect members of parliament (MPs) to the House of Commons, who then form the government or opposition party. The leader of the party with the most MPs becomes the Prime Minister, who serves as the head of government. The monarch serves as the head of state, but largely performs ceremonial duties. The Prime Minister and the cabinet are accountable to the parliament and can be removed through a vote of no confidence. The parliament is responsible for passing laws, approving the budget, and scrutinizing the government's actions. Other examples of parliamentary democracies include Canada, Australia, and United Kingdom.

5. **Constitutional democracy:** This system is based on a written constitution that sets out the fundamental principles and rules governing the political system. The constitution usually establishes the limits of government power and protects individual rights and freedoms.

   Germany is an example of a constitutional democracy. In this system, the country has a written constitution, known as the Basic Law, which outlines the rights and responsibilities of citizens and the government. The constitution is the supreme law of the land and all laws and government actions must be in accordance with it. Germany has a federal system, with power divided between the federal government and the 16 states. Citizens have the right to vote in free and fair elections, and there are checks and balances in place to prevent any one branch of government from becoming too powerful. Other examples of constitutional democracies include the United States, Japan, and South Africa.

6. **Hybrid democracy:** This is a combination of two or more types of democracy. For example, a presidential democracy may have some elements of direct democracy, such as referendums or citizen initiatives.

   For example, in Russia is the country has elements of both democratic and authoritarian governance. While the country has regular elections, the government has been accused of suppressing opposition parties and independent media. The president has significant executive power, including the ability to dissolve the parliament and appoint judges. The government has also been accused of human rights abuses and restrictions on civil liberties. Other examples of hybrid democracies include Turkey, Venezuela, and Hungary.

   It's worth noting that these different types of democracy are not mutually exclusive, and many countries have blended elements of different types to create unique systems of governance.

2

Principles and Dimensions of Democracy

The Principles of Democracy

Democracy is a form of government in which power is vested in the people, who exercise that power either directly or through representatives. The principles of democracy are a set of fundamental values and beliefs that are essential to the functioning of a democratic society. These principles are intended to ensure that the government is answerable to the people, that individual rights and liberties are protected, and that all citizens have an equal say in decision-making.

The principles of democracy include popular sovereignty, the rule of law, separation of powers, protection of individual rights and liberties, accountability and transparency, pluralism, civil society, and political tolerance. These principles form the foundation of democratic governance and are essential to ensuring that government is responsive to the needs and desires of the people. While the specific implementation of democratic principles can vary from country to country, they are generally seen as essential to a healthy democracy. By upholding these principles, democratic societies are able to promote freedom, equality, and justice, and to provide opportunities for all citizens to participate in the decision-making process.

The principles of democracy can vary depending on the context and the political system in question, but generally include the following:

Popular Sovereignty

The ultimate source of political power is the people, who are able to participate in the decision-making process through free and fair elections. Popular sovereignty is the principle that the people are the ultimate source of political power in a democratic society. This means that the government derives its authority from the people and is accountable to them for its actions. In a system of popular sovereignty, the people have the right to participate in the decision-making process through free and fair elections, as well as through other forms of direct or indirect participation, such as referendums, petitions, or protests.

The idea of popular sovereignty is based on the belief that government should be of the people, by the people, and for the people. It is a key element of democratic governance, as it ensures that the government is responsive to the needs and desires of the people it serves. It also helps to promote political stability and legitimacy, as people are more likely to accept the decisions of a government that they feel represents their interests. While popular sovereignty is a fundamental principle of democracy, it can also pose challenges. For example, ensuring that everyone's voice is heard and that decisions reflect the will of the majority without infringing on the rights of minorities can be difficult. However, by upholding the principle of popular sovereignty, democratic societies can ensure that the government is accountable to the people and that their voices are heard in the decision-making process.

Rule of Law

All individuals, including government officials, are subject to and must abide by the law. The rule of law is a principle that states that all individuals and entities, including government officials, are subject to and must abide by the law. This means that no one is above the law, and that all individuals are entitled to the same legal protections and procedures. The rule of law is a fundamental principle of democratic governance, as it ensures that government officials are held accountable for their actions and that citizens have confidence in the fairness and impartiality of the legal system.

The rule of law requires that laws are clear, predictable, and applied consistently. It also requires that laws are enforced fairly and without discrimination, and that legal disputes are resolved through a transparent and impartial process. In addition, the rule of law requires that the government operates within the framework of the constitution and that the rights and freedoms of citizens are protected. By upholding the principle of the rule of law, democratic societies can promote justice, equality, and the protection of individual rights and freedoms. It also helps to ensure that the government operates in a transparent and accountable manner, and that citizens have confidence in the legal system. However, ensuring the rule of law can be challenging, particularly in contexts where corruption, discrimination, or other factors may undermine the impartiality and effectiveness of the legal system.

Separation of Powers

Power is divided among different branches of government, such as the legislative, executive, and judicial branches, in order to prevent any one branch from becoming too powerful. Separation of powers is the principle that political power should be divided among different branches of government in order to prevent any one branch from becoming too powerful. This means that power is distributed among the legislative, executive, and judicial branches of government, each of which has its own distinct responsibilities and functions.

The legislative branch, which is typically composed of elected representatives, is responsible for creating laws. The executive branch, which is typically headed by a president or prime minister, is responsible for enforcing laws and managing the day-to-day operations of government. The judicial branch, which is typically composed of judges and other legal professionals, is responsible for interpreting the law and adjudicating legal disputes.

The separation of powers is a fundamental principle of democratic governance, as it helps to ensure that no single branch of government becomes too powerful and that each branch is able to check the power of the others. By ensuring a system of checks and balances, the separation of powers can help to prevent abuses of power, corruption, and other forms of tyranny. However, ensuring a functional system of separation of powers can be challenging, particularly in contexts where there is significant political polarization, corruption, or other factors that may undermine the effectiveness and impartiality of the government. Nevertheless, by upholding the principle of separation of powers, democratic societies can promote stability, accountability, and the protection of individual rights and freedoms.

Protection of Individual Rights and Liberties

Citizens are guaranteed certain rights and freedoms, such as freedom of speech, religion, and the press, as well as the right to a fair trial. Protection of individual rights and liberties is a fundamental principle of democratic governance, which ensures that individuals have the freedom to pursue their own goals and interests without undue interference from the government or other entities. This principle recognizes that each individual has inherent dignity and worth, and is entitled to basic human rights such as freedom of speech, freedom of assembly, freedom of religion, and the right to due process of law. In a democratic society, the protection of individual rights and liberties is enshrined in the constitution or other legal documents, and is enforced by the judicial system. This means that individuals have the right to challenge any violations of their rights in court, and that the government is bound by law to respect and protect these rights.

The protection of individual rights and liberties is essential to ensuring that democratic societies are able to promote freedom, equality, and justice. It helps to ensure that individuals are able to express themselves freely, to participate in the decision-making process, and to live their lives without fear of persecution or discrimination. It also helps to prevent abuses of power and ensures that the government is held accountable to the people it serves. However, ensuring the protection of individual rights and liberties can be challenging, particularly in contexts where there is significant political polarization, discrimination, or other factors that may undermine the rights of certain individuals or groups. Nevertheless, by upholding the principle of protection of individual rights and liberties, democratic societies can promote human dignity, respect, and equality for all.

Accountability and Transparency

Government officials and institutions are held accountable to the people through regular elections, public hearings, and other forms of oversight. Accountability and transparency are fundamental principles of democratic governance, which ensure that the government is accountable to the people it serves and operates in a transparent and accountable manner. Accountability refers to the responsibility of government officials to act in the best interests of the public and to answer for their actions if they fail to do so. Transparency refers to the openness of government operations and decision-making, and the ability of citizens to access information about government activities.

In a democratic society, accountability and transparency are ensured through a number of mechanisms, including free and fair elections, independent media, and oversight by civil society organizations and government watchdogs. The government is accountable to the people through regular elections, and officials are held accountable for their actions through impeachment, recall, or other legal means. Transparency is ensured through freedom of information laws, public hearings, and open meetings, which allow citizens to access information about government activities and participate in the decision-making process. The principles of accountability and transparency are essential to ensuring that the government operates in the best interests of the public and that citizens have confidence in the legitimacy and effectiveness of the government. They help to prevent corruption, abuse of power, and other forms of malfeasance, and promote transparency and public trust in government institutions.

However, ensuring accountability and transparency can be challenging, particularly in contexts where there is significant political polarization, corruption, or other factors that may undermine the impartiality and effectiveness of the government. Nevertheless, by upholding the principles of accountability and transparency, democratic societies can promote fairness, justice, and the protection of individual rights and freedoms.

Pluralism

A variety of voices and perspectives are welcomed and encouraged in the political process, and individuals are free to organize and associate with others who share their views. Pluralism recognizes that a diverse society will naturally have a range of different views, interests, and perspectives. This principle asserts that a democratic society should accommodate this diversity by allowing multiple groups to participate in the decision-making process and by ensuring that each group is able to have its voice heard. In a pluralistic society, individuals and groups are free to express their opinions and to participate in the political process through a range of mechanisms, such as political parties, interest groups, and social movements. This helps to ensure that different perspectives and interests are represented in the political process, and that the government is responsive to the needs and desires of a diverse citizenry.

The principle of pluralism is essential to ensuring that democratic societies are inclusive and representative, and that individuals are able to express their opinions and participate in the decision-making process. It helps to prevent the dominance of a single group or perspective, and promotes the inclusion of marginalized or underrepresented groups in the political process. However, ensuring pluralism can be challenging, particularly in contexts where there is significant political polarization or where certain groups face discrimination or marginalization. Nevertheless, by upholding the principle of pluralism, democratic societies can promote diversity, inclusivity, and the protection of individual rights and freedoms.

Civil Society

The existence of an active and engaged civil society, made up of independent organizations and associations, is seen as essential to a healthy democracy.

Civil society is an essential component of democratic governance, which refers to the space and mechanisms outside of the government and the private sector, where citizens can organize, mobilize and engage in activities to promote the public interest. Civil society is made up of a range of non-governmental organizations, community groups, social movements, and other forms of civic organizations that represent the interests and concerns of citizens.

In a democratic society, civil society serves as a vital check on the power of the government and private sector, and helps to promote transparency, accountability, and responsiveness. Civil society organizations can monitor the actions of the government and private sector, provide alternative policy proposals, and mobilize citizens to participate in the decision-making process.

Civil society organizations also play a crucial role in promoting human rights, social justice, and environmental protection. Civil society is essential to ensuring that democratic societies are inclusive and representative, and that citizens have a meaningful voice in the decision-making process. It helps to foster a culture of active citizenship, and promotes public engagement in democratic processes. However, ensuring a strong and vibrant civil society can be challenging, particularly in contexts where there is limited space for civil society to operate, or where civil society organizations face harassment or persecution. Nevertheless, by upholding the principle of civil society, democratic societies can promote diversity, inclusivity, and the protection of individual rights and freedoms.

Political Tolerance

The willingness to tolerate opposing views and perspectives, even if one strongly disagrees with them, is necessary for democratic discourse and decision-making. Political tolerance is an important principle of democratic governance, which refers to the willingness of individuals and groups to accept and respect the rights and opinions of those with whom they disagree politically. It is the ability to tolerate and accept political differences and to engage in constructive dialogue and debate, without resorting to violence, coercion, or discrimination.

In a democratic society, political tolerance is essential to promoting peaceful coexistence and the protection of individual rights and freedoms. It allows individuals and groups with different political perspectives to engage in a constructive dialogue, without fear of retaliation or persecution. It also promotes mutual respect and understanding, and helps to prevent the escalation of political conflicts into violence or other forms of destructive behavior. Political tolerance is particularly important in societies that are characterized by diversity and polarization, where there may be significant differences in political beliefs, ideologies, and identities. In such contexts, political tolerance helps to promote social cohesion and to prevent the exclusion and marginalization of certain groups or individuals. However, political tolerance can be challenging to uphold in contexts where there is significant political polarization, social conflict, or other factors that may undermine trust and respect between individuals and groups. Nevertheless, by upholding the principle of political tolerance, democratic societies can promote peaceful coexistence, social cohesion, and the protection of individual rights and freedoms.

Respect for Human Dignity

The principle of respect for human dignity is a fundamental aspect of democracy. It emphasizes the recognition and protection of the inherent worth and value of every individual in society. In a democratic system, all individuals, regardless of their background, status, or characteristics, are entitled to equal respect, dignity, and treatment under the law.

Respecting human dignity in democracy means recognizing the inherent worth, rights, and equality of every person. It promotes a society that values diversity, inclusivity, justice, and compassion, fostering an environment where individuals can flourish, express themselves freely, and participate fully in shaping their own lives and the collective future of the nation.

Dimensions of Democracy

Social Dimension of democracy

The social dimension of democracy refers to the idea that democratic governments should not only ensure political rights and freedoms, but also work to promote social justice and equality for all citizens. This means that democracy should not be limited to the mere exercise of political power, but should also include a commitment to addressing social and economic issues that affect people's lives. In a socially-oriented democratic system, citizens have the right to access basic services such as education, healthcare, and social security. They also have the right to participate in decisions that affect their lives, such as the formulation of social policies, the allocation of resources, and the regulation of markets.

Moreover, social democracy emphasizes the role of government in promoting social and economic equality through policies such as progressive taxation, income redistribution, and public provision of basic services. The aim is to ensure that everyone has access to the resources and opportunities necessary to live a dignified life. The social dimension of democracy recognizes that freedom and social justice are mutually reinforcing, and that a truly democratic system must strive to achieve both.

Political Dimension of democracy

The political dimension of democracy refers to the set of principles and practices that ensure the exercise of political power is based on the will of the people, and that political decision-making processes are open, transparent, and accountable to citizens.

The core elements of the political dimension of democracy include:

Free and fair elections: Democratic systems require regular, free, and fair elections, in which citizens have the right to vote and to stand for office. Elections should be conducted in a manner that is transparent, impartial, and ensures the secret ballot.

Rule of law: Democratic systems are built on the rule of law, which means that no one, including those in power, is above the law. Laws should be enacted and enforced fairly and consistently, and the judiciary should be independent and impartial.

Separation of powers: Democratic systems are based on the principle of separation of powers, which means that the executive, legislative, and judicial branches of government should be independent of each other and exercise checks and balances on each other's power.

Freedom of expression: Democratic systems require the protection of the freedom of expression, including the press, speech, and assembly. Citizens must have the right to express their opinions and ideas, without fear of retribution.

Citizen participation: Democratic systems require citizen participation in decision-making processes, including the right to petition the government, freedom of association, and the right to form political parties.

The political dimension of democracy is focused on ensuring that citizens have the right to participate in the political process and that those in power are accountable to the people they serve.

Economic Dimension of Democracy

The economic dimension of democracy refers to the principles and practices that promote economic freedom, equity, and prosperity within a democratic system. A democratic system that promotes economic freedom ensures that citizens have the right to participate in economic activities without undue restrictions or discrimination. The economic dimension of democracy emphasizes the importance of promoting economic freedom, equity, and prosperity within a democratic system, and of ensuring that economic policies and practices are transparent, accountable, and responsive to the needs and aspirations of citizens.

The core elements of the economic dimension of democracy include:

Market economy: Democratic systems often promote a market economy, which allows individuals to engage in economic activities freely and without interference. This includes the right to own and control property, to establish and operate businesses, and to buy and sell goods and services in a competitive market.

Economic policies: Democratic systems establish economic policies that promote economic growth, equity, and stability. Such policies may include investment in infrastructure, education, and research and development; progressive taxation; social safety nets; and regulations to ensure fair competition and prevent monopolies.

Workers' rights: Democratic systems also promote workers' rights, including the right to form and join unions, to bargain collectively, and to strike. Workers are also protected from exploitation and discrimination, and they are entitled to safe working conditions and fair compensation.

Protection of property rights: Democratic systems protect property rights, including intellectual property, by ensuring that citizens have the right to own and control their property, and that their property is protected from theft, fraud, or expropriation by the government or other private entities.

Access to credit: Democratic systems also promote access to credit, including microcredit and other forms of financial support, especially for marginalized groups and entrepreneurs.

3

Democracy and Decentralization

Features of Democracy

Democracy is a form of government in which the people have the power to participate in the decision-making process. There are several features of democracy which can helps in the determination of working of Government. The features of democracy ensure that the government is accountable to the people, and that individual rights are protected. These are explained below:

- ***Free and fair elections:*** Elections are the cornerstone of democracy, and free and fair elections are crucial to ensuring that the people have a say in the government.
- ***Rule of law:*** The rule of law means that everyone, including the government, is subject to the law. This principle ensures that no one is above the law, and that everyone is held accountable for their actions.
- ***Protection of individual rights***: Democracies protect the individual rights of their citizens, including freedom of speech, freedom of assembly, freedom of religion, and freedom of the press.
- ***Separation of powers:*** Democracies typically have a system of checks and balances that prevents any one branch of government from becoming too powerful. This separation of powers ensures that no one person or group has too much control.
- ***Independent judiciary:*** Democracies have an independent judiciary that is free from political interference. This ensures that the law is applied fairly and impartially.
- ***Decentralization of power:*** Democracies often have a decentralized system of government, which means that power is distributed among different levels of government. This helps to prevent the concentration of power in the hands of a few individuals or groups.
- ***Civil society participation:*** In a democracy, civil society groups play an important role in holding the government accountable and representing the interests of different segments of society.

Democracy Decentralization

Democratic decentralization refers to the process of devolving power and decision-making authority from the central government to local and regional levels of government. This involves the transfer of political, administrative, and fiscal responsibilities to sub-national levels of government, such as states, provinces, or municipalities.

The purpose of democratic decentralization is to bring decision-making closer to the people and to promote greater participation and engagement in the governance process. It is also intended to improve the effectiveness and efficiency of public services by tailoring them to the specific needs of local communities. Democratic decentralization can take many different forms, depending on the specific political, economic, and social context. It may involve the creation of new local governments, the transfer of powers from central to local government, or the strengthening of existing local government institutions.

Following features collectively contribute to the essence of democratic decentralization, promoting citizen participation, accountability, and responsive governance at the local level while maintaining the overall democratic framework of the country.

Features of Decentralization

1. **Devolution of power:** Devolution of power is a crucial aspect of democratic decentralization, involving the transfer of political authority from central governments to lower levels of governance. It aims to distribute power evenly, empower local communities, and enhance governance effectiveness. Devolution entails transferring specific powers and responsibilities to regional or local authorities, covering areas such as governance, public services, infrastructure, education, healthcare, and economic development. It provides autonomy to regional or local authorities within national laws and policies, enabling them to respond effectively to community needs. By shifting decision-making to local levels, devolution ensures more responsive and context-specific governance, promoting citizen participation and meeting diverse community needs. Overall, devolution strengthens democracy by sharing power and catering to the varied requirements of communities.
2. **Subsidiarity principle:** The subsidiarity principle guides decision-making in democratic decentralization, promoting local autonomy and addressing local needs. It emphasizes decision-making at the appropriate level, closer to affected populations, rather than centralizing power.

The principle recognizes the understanding and capabilities of local authorities in addressing specific community challenges. It balances centralized decision-making and local autonomy, fostering participatory governance. Local authorities possess contextual knowledge and engage directly with citizens.

Decentralizing power enables swift responses to local needs and fosters accountability. It encourages citizen participation in shaping local policies and programs. Checks and balances are necessary within national frameworks. Accountability, transparency, and coordination ensure effective governance.

3. **Participatory decision making:** Participatory decision-making not only promotes inclusivity but also fosters a sense of ownership and shared responsibility among participants. By involving citizens in the decision-making process, it strengthens social cohesion and trust in local institutions. Moreover, participatory approaches enable the identification of innovative solutions and harness local expertise, leading to more effective and sustainable outcomes. It also serves as a platform for capacity building, enabling citizens to develop skills in critical thinking, problem-solving, and civic engagement. Overall, participatory decision-making empowers communities, strengthens democracy, and contributes to more equitable and impactful local governance.
4. **Local Responsiveness:** The local responsiveness of democratic decentralization refers to how well decentralized governance systems can meet the needs of the people they serve. It depends on creating an environment that supports local autonomy, citizen participation, accountability, and effective feedback. When these factors are in place, decentralized systems can better address the specific needs and desires of local communities. Democratic decentralization aims to give more power and resources to local governments and communities so they can play a bigger role in making decisions and implementing programs that directly affect them. This approach enhances responsiveness and ensures that governance is more in tune with the needs of local populations.
5. **Local Accountability:** Ensuring local accountability is crucial in democratic decentralization as it holds decentralized institutions and authorities responsible for their actions and use of resources. It involves establishing clear legal frameworks and mechanisms, while also building the capacity of decentralized institutions. Accountability promotes transparency, preventing corruption and misuse of funds. It fosters good governance, adherence to laws, and ethical standards. By

being accountable, decentralized authorities gain trust and confidence from the public, encouraging citizen participation. Accountability also allows citizens to assess and influence the quality of public services, leading to improved outcomes in service delivery.

6. **Transparency and Openness:** Transparency in government means being open, accountable, and responsive to the public. It involves providing citizens with access to information, allowing them to participate and influence decisions. Transparency prevents corruption and builds trust in government. It includes publishing reports, granting public access to information, and disclosing funding sources. In an open democracy, citizens have a say, and decisions align with democratic principles and human rights. Achieving transparency requires commitment from governments to create an enabling environment, establish accountability mechanisms, and promote openness in decision-making and resource allocation.
7. **Enhancing the Flow of Information:** Promoting the flow of information is vital in democratic decentralization for transparency, citizen engagement, and effective decision-making. Strategies to achieve this include enacting access to information laws, establishing channels for disseminating information, conducting public consultations, facilitating citizen participation, promoting civic education, leveraging technology, enhancing capacity, establishing feedback mechanisms, and fostering partnerships. These measures ensure that relevant information is accessible, citizens have opportunities to provide input, and decentralized institutions are held accountable.
8. **Capacity-Building and Institutional Development:** Capacity-building focuses on enhancing the knowledge, skills, and abilities of individuals and organizations involved in local governance, while institutional development aims to strengthen the structures, systems, and processes within local authorities. These efforts empower local officials, staff, and community leaders to effectively carry out their responsibilities and deliver services to their communities. By building capacity and developing institutions, democratic decentralization promotes effective decision-making, improved service delivery, and increased citizen participation at the local level, contributing to a more robust and inclusive democratic system.
9. **Equity and Social Inclusion:** In democratic decentralization, equity and social inclusion are important aspects. This means that decisions and resources should be distributed fairly and in a way that considers

the needs of all people, especially those who have been marginalized or face disadvantages. Democratic decentralization aims to give everyone a voice in local decision-making and ensure that public services are accessible to all. By focusing on equity and social inclusion, democratic decentralization aims to reduce inequalities and create a society where everyone has equal opportunities and benefits from development. This helps to bring people together, address disparities, and create a fair and inclusive community.

10. **Democratic Values and Human Rights:** Democratic decentralization encompasses democratic values and human rights as essential features. It promotes inclusive and accountable decision-making processes that empower citizens to actively participate in shaping policies and programs. By upholding democratic values, such as equality, freedom, and citizen engagement, democratic decentralization strengthens democratic legitimacy and fosters a sense of ownership among individuals. Moreover, it prioritizes the protection and promotion of human rights, ensuring that all individuals, regardless of their background, have their rights respected and upheld. Through the integration of democratic values and human rights, democratic decentralization creates a fair, equitable, and inclusive society that addresses social inequalities and promotes social justice at the local level.

Advantages of Democratic Decentralization

Democratic decentralization offers numerous advantages, which includes the following:

- ***Improved governance:*** Democratic decentralization fosters improved governance by granting citizens a greater role in determining the functioning of their communities. Consequently, governments become more responsive and accountable.
- ***Enhanced efficiency:*** Democratic decentralization promotes increased efficiency since local governments tend to be more efficient compared to centralized ones. This is primarily due to their proximity to the people they serve and their better understanding of local needs.
- ***Greater participation:*** Democratic decentralization encourages greater citizen participation by providing opportunities for involvement in decision-making processes at the local level. This contributes to the development of a society that values civic engagement.
- ***Heightened responsiveness:*** Democratic decentralization leads to heightened responsiveness as local governments possess a greater

awareness of the challenges faced by their citizens and can take swift action to address them.

Challenges of Democratic Decentralization

Nonetheless, democratic decentralization also presents certain challenges, which include the following:

- ***Cost implications:*** Democratic decentralization can be financially burdensome as it necessitates the establishment of new institutions and the allocation of resources from the central government to local governments.
- ***Capacity constraints:*** Local governments may lack the capacity to effectively manage the responsibilities transferred to them, leading to issues like corruption and inefficiency.
- ***Potential conflicts:*** Democratic decentralization can result in conflicts as different groups compete for power and resources. Managing such conflicts can be particularly challenging in countries with a history of ethnic or religious tensions.

Despite these challenges, democratic decentralization remains a valuable tool for enhancing governance and fostering a more democratic society.

4

Fundamental Rights in the Indian Constitution

The fundamental rights enshrined in the Constitution of India are a cornerstone of the country's democratic framework, guaranteeing essential protections and liberties to its citizens. These rights, often referred to as the "heart and soul" of the Constitution, reflect the deep commitment of the framers to create a just and inclusive society. The Constitution, adopted on January 26, 1950, sets forth a comprehensive set of fundamental rights that safeguard individual autonomy, promote equality, and protect against discrimination and abuse of power.

Irrespective of their caste, ethnicity, location of birth, religion, or gender, all Indian people are guaranteed certain fundamental rights under Part III of the Indian Constitution. These fundamental rights are referred to as justified fundamental rights. These were referred to by Dr. B. R. Ambedkar as the parts of the constitution that most directly affected citizens. These are seen as being a crucial component of the constitution because they guard the liberties and rights of the people of the nation from any abuse or intrusion by the government, which in a democracy has the authority to do so. These are the negative responsibilities that the government and people have. These rights try to achieve the goals set out in the Preamble, of justice, liberty, equality, fraternity, and dignity.

India's fundamental rights encompass a wide range of civil, political, social, and economic rights that are essential for the dignity, well-being, and freedom of its citizens. They include the right to equality before the law, the right to freedom of speech and expression, the right to practice one's religion, the right to protection from discrimination, the right to life and personal liberty, and the right to education and social security, among others. These rights are not only legally protected but also represent the moral and ethical principles that underpin a democratic society.

The framers of the Indian Constitution were deeply influenced by the Universal Declaration of Human Rights and sought to create a comprehensive framework of rights that would empower individuals and protect them from arbitrary state action. These rights not only enable citizens to participate actively in the democratic process but also serve as safeguards against any form of oppression or injustice. They ensure that all individuals, regardless of their background or status, have equal opportunities, dignity, and protection under the law.

Over the years, the Indian judiciary has played a crucial role in interpreting and upholding these fundamental rights, ensuring their effective implementation and enforcement. The Supreme Court of India, through its landmark judgments, has expanded and strengthened the scope of these rights, paving the way for greater inclusivity, social justice, and protection of individual liberties.

However, it is important to recognize that the exercise of fundamental rights is not absolute and can be subject to reasonable restrictions in certain circumstances, such as public order, morality, or the protection of national security. Balancing individual rights with the collective welfare of society is a delicate task that requires thoughtful consideration and a commitment to upholding the principles of justice and fairness.

Fundamental Rights

1. Right to Equality: (Article 14 to 18)

Democracy can prosper and blossom only in a society where all individuals are treated fairly and without any form of discrimination. In order to remove the barrier of current social and economic inequalities and enable the varied populations of the country to enjoy the rights and liberties provided by the constitution, it was felt by the Constitution's drafters to include such a clause. Eliminating inequalities based on religion, social conventions, and long-standing customs like untouchability, casteism, racial discrimination, etc. that are still practiced in some parts of India was considered crucial. The articles related to right to equality are explained as follows,

Article 14: Equality Before Law: Asserts that every individual, regardless of their citizenship, nationality, or legal status, shall receive equal treatment under the law and equal protection of their rights within the borders of India. This right extends to all persons, including citizens, foreigners, corporate entities, registered societies, or any other legal entities.

Article 15: Prohibition of Discrimination: Guarantees that no citizen will be subject to discrimination solely based on their location of birth, race, caste, or religion.

Article 16: Equality of Opportunity in Public Employment: The Indian constitution ensures that all citizens have an equal chance and fair opportunity when it comes to employment or appointment to any public position.

Article 17: Abolition of Untouchability: abolishes "untouchability" and outlaws its use in any way. Any disability imposed as a result of untouchability is illegal and will be punished accordingly. A person who has been found guilty of the "untouchability" offence is ineligible to run for office in the federal or state legislatures. The offences include, refusing to permit any individual entry into any store, hotel, public place of worship, or location of public entertainment, refusing to let anyone into hospitals, educational institutions, or hostels set up for the benefit of the public, offering traditional, religious, philosophical, or any other forms of justifications for the practice of untouchability, or directly or indirectly endorsing untouchability.

Article 18: Abolition of Titles: No Indian citizen can be granted any titles like "Raja" (King), "Maharaja" (Great King), "Nawab" (Noble), "Rani" (Queen), "Maharani" (Great Queen), "Sir," and "Sardar" (Chief). These titles were often associated with social status, hereditary privileges, or specific roles in society. The purpose of this provision is to promote equality among citizens and discourage the practice of bestowing titles based on social or hereditary considerations.

Titles are abolished by Article 18 of the Indian Constitution, which also contains the following four provisions:

- Except for a military or scholarly distinction, it forbids the state from bestowing any titles on either citizens or visitors.
- A citizen of India is not permitted to accept any titles from any foreign state.
- A foreigner who holds a position of profit or trust on behalf of the state is not permitted to take a title from another foreign state without the president of India's permission.
- Without the president's approval, no citizen or foreigner holding an office of profit or trust inside the borders of India is permitted to accept a gift, emolument, or position from or under a foreign State.

2. Right to Freedom: (Article 19 to 22)

The Indian Constitution defines the right to freedom as the essential liberties guaranteed by Articles 19 to 22. The purpose of these rights is to advance the ideals of liberty in order to eliminate individual inequities and grant everyone the right to live a life of dignity. The essence of "freedom" lies in the absence of restrictions. It encompasses various rights such as the freedom to move, speak and express oneself, practice religion, travel, work, define one's own identity, and own property. The government should minimize its interference in individual affairs to ensure the provision of these rights. It should serve as a foundation for the state, allowing its citizens to enjoy these fundamental liberties. These freedoms, considered essential in any democratic country, are explicitly recognized as fundamental rights in the Constitution, even within a democratic nation like India. Following articles elaborates the right to freedom as follows.

Article 19: Protection of Six Rights: All citizens are guaranteed six freedoms, including:

- **Right to freedom of speech and expression:** Freedom to express personal views, opinions, beliefs, and convictions without restrictions using verbal communication, written form, printing, imagery, or any other means of expression.
- **Right to assemble peaceably and without arms:** This right includes the freedom to arrange public meetings, protests, and parades, but only in public areas. However, it does not protect gatherings that turn violent, disorderly, or riotous, nor does it cover strikes.
- **Right to form associations or unions or co-operative societies:** This right allows individuals to create or choose not to create political parties, companies, partnerships, societies, clubs, organizations, trade unions, or any other types of groups.
- **Right to move freely throughout the territory of India:** The freedom to move has two aspects: internal freedom (the right to travel within the country) covered by Article 19, and external freedom (the right to leave the country and return) covered by Article 21.
- **Right to reside and settle in any part of the territory of India:** To preserve the unique culture, customs, traditional livelihoods, and property of tribes, restrictions are imposed on outsiders to live and settle in tribal areas. This is done to prevent the exploitation of these communities and ensure the preservation of their way of life.
- **Right to practice any profession or to carry on any occupation, trade or business:** The right to engage in any profession, occupation, trade, or business allows individuals the freedom to choose and pursue their desired career paths and economic activities without unnecessary restrictions or discrimination. The right does not cover engaging in professions that are considered immoral, such as trafficking in women or children, or occupations that pose a threat to public safety, like dealing with harmful drugs or explosives.

Article 20: Protection in Respect of Conviction for Offences: This provision protects individuals, including citizens, foreigners, and legal entities like companies or corporations, from unjust and excessive punishment. It ensures that a person cannot be convicted of an act unless it is in violation of a law existing at the time of the act, and they cannot face a penalty greater than what the law prescribes. Double jeopardy is prohibited, meaning a person cannot be prosecuted or punished multiple times for the same offense. Additionally, no person accused of a crime can be forced to testify against themselves.

Article 21: Protection of Life and Personal Liberty: This provision states that no individual, whether a citizen or non-citizen, can be deprived of their life or personal liberty unless it is done in accordance with established legal procedures. The right to life encompasses more than mere survival and includes the right to live with dignity and fulfillment, encompassing all aspects that contribute to a meaningful and worthwhile existence.

Article 22: Protection Against Arrest and Detention: This article provides protection to individuals who are arrested or detained. Detention can be punitive (after trial and conviction) or preventive (without trial and conviction). The first part of Article 22 ensures certain rights to individuals, including being informed of the reasons for arrest, the right to consult and be defended by a lawyer, and being brought before a magistrate within 24 hours. Unless authorized by the magistrate, the person must be released after 24 hours. The second part of Article 22 pertains to preventive detention and applies to both citizens and non-citizens. It establishes that detention cannot exceed three months unless a board of judges reports sufficient cause for an extended detention. The grounds of detention must be communicated to the person, who should also be given an opportunity to challenge the detention order.

Article 22(A): Right to Education: provision mandates that the State must offer free and compulsory education to all children aged six to fourteen. However, this right specifically applies to elementary education and does not encompass higher or professional education. This provision was introduced through the 86th Constitutional Amendment Act in 2002. Prior to this amendment, the Constitution included a provision for free and compulsory education for children under Article 45 in Part IV of the constitution.

3. Right against exploitation: (Article 23 to 24)

Indian law forbids slavery and any other practice that violates a person's freedom and dignity. However, there are people who still view themselves as superior to others. As a result, millions of women and children fall prey to human trafficking and are compelled to work against their will for low wages.

Human dignity is guaranteed by the right against exploitation, which is protected under Articles 23 and 24 of the Indian Constitution. preserving the freedom and human dignity that the Indian Constitution was foun ded on. Following articles of the Indian constitution portrays the right against exploitations,

Article 23: Prohibition of Human Trafficking and Forced Labour: This Article is aimed at preventing human trafficking and forced labor, specifically beggary, in order to protect the rights of marginalized and disadvantaged individuals in the country. This right applies to both Indian citizens and non-citizens. It prohibits various forms of human trafficking, including the sale and purchase of men, women, and children, involvement in prostitution, the practice of Devadasis, and slavery. The Immoral Traffic (Prevention) Act of 1956 has been enacted to address violations of this fundamental right.

Article 24: Prohibition of Child Labour: Article 24 of the Indian Constitution prohibits the employment of children below the age of 14 in hazardous occupations such as factories and mines. However, it does not restrict their employment in harmless or non-hazardous work. The Child Labour (Prohibition and Regulation) Act of 1986 (renamed as Child & Adolescent Labour (Prohibition and Regulation) Act in 2016) addresses violations related to this right. The 2016 amendment completely bans the employment of children below 14 years in all occupations and processes, and also prohibits the employment of adolescents (14-18 years) in hazardous occupations or processes.

4. Right to freedom of religion: (Article 25 to 28)

Religion holds significant importance in the lives of people in India, and the Indian Constitution acknowledges this by providing the right to freedom of religion through Articles 25 to 28. The Constitution promotes a secular model, ensuring that every individual has the freedom to choose and practice their own religion. Secularism is considered a fundamental principle of the Constitution, as established in the Kesavananda Bharati case. Islam, Hinduism, Jainism, Buddhism, Sikhism, and Christianity are the primary religions practiced in India. Religion-specific laws exist in the country, and Goa is the only state with a Uniform Civil Code known as the Goa Civil Code. The Constitution encourages religious harmony, fostering love and respect for various religions across the country. Articles related to right to freedom of religion explained below.

Article 25: Freedom of Conscience, Profession, Practice and Propagation: This article grants individuals the freedom of conscience to have their own beliefs, the right to profess and practice any religion, and the freedom to propagate their religion. These rights extend to both citizens and non-citizens. The freedom of conscience allows one to choose whether or not to follow a religion. The right to profess enables individuals to openly declare their religious beliefs and faith. The right to practice encompasses engaging in religious rituals, ceremonies, and expressing one's beliefs. The right to propagate permits the spreading of information about one's religion and attracting others to it, but it does not allow for forced conversions.

Article 26: Freedom to Manage Religious Affairs: Article 26 grants every religious denomination, or a specific section of it, the right to establish and maintain institutions for religious and charitable purposes. It also empowers religious denominations to independently manage their own religious affairs. Additionally, religious denominations have the right to own and acquire movable and immovable property, and they have the authority to administer such property. However, these rights are subject to considerations of public order, morality, and health.

Article 27: Freedom from Taxation for Promotion of a Religion: This article states that no individual can be compelled to pay taxes for the promotion or maintenance of any specific religion or religious denomination. It further specifies that public funds, collected through taxes, cannot be utilized to promote or support any particular religion. The Constitution prohibits any form of favoritism, patronage, or support towards one religion over others. It specifically addresses the levy of taxes and not fees. Fees may be imposed for the secular administration of religious institutions rather than for the promotion or maintenance of religion.

Article 28: Freedom from Attending Religious Instruction: This article of the Indian Constitution stipulates that no religious instruction should be provided in educational institutions that are fully funded by the government (State funds). However, this provision does not apply to educational institutions that are administered by the State or established under an endowment or trust. Furthermore, no individual can be compelled to attend religious instructions or participate in worship without their consent in educational institutions recognized by the State or receiving financial assistance from the government. In the case of a minor, the consent of their guardian is required.

5. Cultural & Educational Rights: (Article 29 & 30)

India, with its diverse population encompassing various races, castes, languages, and cultures, places significant importance on safeguarding the rights of minorities. Article 29 and 30 of the Indian Constitution specifically address the rights related to culture and education to ensure the protection of any section of citizens across different parts of the country, including those with diverse languages, scripts, and cultures. The cultural and educational rights guaranteed by Article 29 are equally available to every citizen, including minorities. These rights empower minority communities to preserve and uphold their distinct cultural identities.

Article 29: Protection of Interests of Minorities: Article 29 ensures the protection of the interests of both minority and majority communities. It guarantees every section of citizens residing in any part of the country the right to safeguard and preserve their distinct language, script, or culture. This provision extends to religious, linguistic, and cultural minorities, but it is not exclusively limited to them. Additionally, Article 29 ensures that no individual citizen can be denied admission into any educational institution solely based on their religion, race, caste, or language. Therefore, Article 29 safeguards the rights of both minority and majority communities in India.

Article 30: Right of Minorities to Establish and Administer Educational Institutions: It ensures that minorities, including religious, cultural, or linguistic groups, have the right to establish and administer educational institutions of their choice. The State is prohibited from discriminating against any educational institution managed by a minority. Additionally, the compensation amount for the compulsory acquisition of any property of a minority educational institution cannot infringe upon their guaranteed rights. This provision was introduced through the 44th Amendment Act in 1978 to safeguard the rights of minorities in this context. It's important to note that Article 30's protection is exclusively limited to minorities and does not extend to other sections of citizens, as covered under Article 29.

Note: Article 31 *of the Indian Constitution, which has been repealed, previously provided for the protection of property rights. It stated that no person could be deprived of their property except by authority of law, and that compensation must be provided for any such deprivation. However, the right to property was removed as a fundamental right and was instead made a legal right by the 44th Amendment Act of 1978.*

6. Right to Constitutional Remedies: (Article 32 to 35)

Article 32 of the Indian Constitution is considered the "soul" and "heart" of the Constitution as it empowers individuals to directly approach the Supreme Court for the enforcement of Fundamental Rights. The Fundamental Rights provided in the Constitution serve as a protective shield, and Article 32 acts as the mechanism to ensure their implementation. It is hailed as a crucial provision that upholds the essence and significance of the Constitution.

Article 32 of the Indian Constitution is widely regarded as the most important article as it grants individuals the right to seek protection and remedies for the enforcement of Fundamental Rights. It establishes the Supreme Court as the authority to issue orders and directions for the protection of these rights. While Parliament can empower other courts, it excludes high courts as they already possess similar powers under Article 226. The right to move the Supreme Court cannot be suspended except in cases of national emergency. Article 32 specifically pertains to the enforcement of Fundamental Rights and does not extend to non-fundamental constitutional rights, statutory rights, or customary rights. The violation of a fundamental right is a prerequisite for invoking the provisions of Article 32.

Article 33 of the Indian Constitution grants Parliament the authority to impose restrictions or curtail the fundamental rights of certain groups such as the Armed Forces, paramilitary forces, police forces, intelligence agencies, and similar entities. This provision aims to ensure that these groups can fulfill their duties effectively and maintain discipline within their ranks. Only Parliament has the power to enact laws under Article 33, and such laws cannot be challenged in court for violating fundamental rights. The term "members of the armed forces" also includes non-combatant employees who provide various services to the armed forces, such as barbers, carpenters, mechanics, cooks, security guards, shoemakers, and tailors.

Article 34 of the Indian Constitution deals with the restrictions on fundamental rights during the imposition of martial law in any area within India. Martial law refers to military rule, which is enforced during extraordinary situations like war, invasion, insurrection, rebellion, riot, or violent resistance to the law. Under Article 34, Parliament has the power to provide compensation (indemnify) to government officials or any other person for their actions related to maintaining or restoring order in the area where martial law is in effect. Any Act of Indemnity passed by Parliament cannot be challenged in court on the grounds of violating fundamental rights.

Article 35 of the Indian Constitution grants exclusive powers to the Parliament to make laws that are necessary to enforce certain fundamental rights. These powers are not given to the state legislatures. The powers of Parliament under Article 35 include:

- Imposing residence requirements for certain employment or appointments in states, union territories, local authorities, or any other authority.
- Authorizing courts other than the Supreme Court and high courts to issue directions, orders, and writs for the protection of fundamental rights.
- Restricting or eliminating the application of fundamental rights for members of armed forces, police forces, and other similar entities.

- Providing compensation (indemnity) to government officials or others for their actions during the imposition of martial law in a particular area.
- Enacting laws to punish offenses such as untouchability, human trafficking, and forced labor.

Article 35 empowers the Parliament to legislate on these matters, even if they fall within the jurisdiction of the state legislatures (State List).

5

Outcomes and Challenges of Democracy

Democracy has been one of the most generally adopted forms of government around the world. Democracy, founded on the values of popular sovereignty, equality, and civic involvement, seeks to give the people political authority. Democracy has had a variety of consequences and impacts on the society and governments that have accepted it throughout history. These outcomes have shaped people's lives, influenced political landscapes, and had far-reaching consequences in the social, economic, and cultural arenas. Ofcourse, democracy may face challenges, its ability to adapt, evolve, and engage citizens in the decision-making process makes it a crucial system for fostering inclusive and prosperous societies. Below, we will explore some of the positive outcomes and challenges before democracy.

Outcomes of Democracy

1. ***Political Stability and Peaceful Power Transitions:*** Democracy provides a way for people to change their government peacefully through regular elections. This allows for the peaceful transfer of power from one government to another, which helps to ensure stability and reduces the risk of authoritarian rule or violent conflict.
2. ***Protection of Individual Rights and Freedoms:*** In a successful democracy, the rights and freedoms of its citizens are protected and respected. It ensures freedom of expression, assembly, and association, allowing individuals to voice their opinions, participate in civic activities, and freely express their ideas without fear of repression or persecution.
3. ***Economic Development:*** Democracies frequently establish a favorable climate for economic growth. Through the promotion of transparency, accountability, and adherence to legal principles, democratic systems entice investments, foster entrepreneurial endeavors, and stimulate innovation. Consequently, this results in economic progress, the generation of employment oppor-tunities, and enhanced living standards for the populace.

4. ***Social Justice and Equality:*** Democracies strive to address social inequalities and promote justice. They provide opportunities for marginalized groups and ensure the inclusion and representation of diverse populations in decision-making processes. Democratic systems work towards reducing discrimination, promoting gender equality, and protecting the rights of minority communities.
5. ***Protection of Human Rights:*** Democracy is closely associated with the protection of human rights. Successful democracies establish legal frameworks and institutions to safeguard civil, political, and socio-economic rights, ensuring the dignity and well-being of all individuals within the society.
6. ***Responsive Governance and Accountability:*** In a successful democracy, government officials and institutions are accountable to the people. Democratic systems encourage transparency, accountability, and responsiveness to the needs and aspirations of the citizens. This leads to more effective governance, as policymakers are held responsible for their actions and decisions.
7. ***Social Cohesion and Inclusive Decision-Making:*** Democracy fosters social cohesion by providing platforms for dialogue, deliberation, and consensus-building. It allows citizens to participate in decision-making processes, ensuring that diverse voices and perspectives are considered. This inclusive approach promotes social harmony, encourages civic engagement, and strengthens the sense of community.
8. ***Protection of the Rule of Law:*** Successful democracies uphold the rule of law, ensuring that laws are applied equally to all citizens. This provides a foundation for a just and fair society, where individuals can seek legal remedies, have access to justice, and have confidence in the legal system.

It is important to note that the outcomes of successful democracies may vary depending on the specific context, history, and socio-political factors of each country.

Challenges Faced by Indian Democracy

While democracy has shown to be a resilient and influential system of governance, it also faces severe implementation and maintenance challenges. These challenges can be caused by internal elements inside a democratic society as well as external forces and influences. Understanding and responding to these issues is critical for the survival and strengthening of democratic institutions and values. From the rise of populism and polarization to issues of corruption and inequality, the challenges faced by democracy require continuous attention and proactive measures to ensure its sustainability.

India is the world's largest democracy, with a population of over 1.3 billion people. However, the country faces a number of challenges to its democracy. Some of the most pressing challenges include:

- **Illiteracy:** Illiteracy hinders meaningful participation in the political process. When a significant portion of the population is unable to read or write, they face barriers in accessing and understanding information related to political issues, candidates, and policies. This lack of literacy limits their ability to make informed decisions and engage in critical thinking regarding government matters. Illiteracy undermines the democratic principle of an informed citizenry and can result in the marginalization of certain groups, leading to unequal representation and decision-making. Efforts to address illiteracy and promote education are vital for empowering individuals to actively participate in democratic processes and contribute to a more inclusive and robust democracy.
- **Poverty:** In impoverished societies, access to basic necessities and opportunities for socioeconomic advancement are limited, leading to inequalities and social unrest. Poverty undermines the ability of citizens to fully participate in the democratic process, as they may lack the resources, education, and time required to engage in political activities or make informed choices. It also creates an environment where individuals are vulnerable to manipulation and exploitation by powerful interests, diminishing the fairness and integrity of democratic systems. Addressing poverty is essential for fostering inclusive and robust democracies that truly represent and uplift all members of society.
- **Casteism:** Casteism undermines the principles of equality, social justice, and inclusion. In societies affected by casteism, individuals are discriminated against and face limited opportunities based on their caste affiliation. This leads to the marginalization and exclusion of certain groups from the democratic process. Caste-based politics and vote bank strategies further exacerbate divisions and hinder the formation of a truly representative and inclusive democracy. Overcoming casteism requires addressing deep-rooted prejudices, promoting social equality, and ensuring equal rights and opportunities for all citizens, irrespective of their caste backgrounds.
- **Corruption:** Corruption distorts the democratic process by compromising free and fair elections. When politicians and officials engage

in corrupt practices, it undermines the integrity of electoral systems and compromises the ability of citizens to choose their representatives freely. Furthermore, corrupt individuals may gain undue influence over policymaking, resulting in policies that prioritize personal interests over the common good. To address the challenge of corruption in democracy, strong anti-corruption measures, including robust legal frameworks, independent judiciary, and effective oversight institutions, are essential. Promoting transparency, accountability, and ethical conduct within public administration and fostering a culture of integrity can help strengthen democratic institutions and restore public trust in the system.

- **Communalism:** Communalism fuels a sense of identity-based polarization and fosters an "us versus them" mentality, leading to the marginalization, discrimination, and exclusion of certain religious or ethnic groups. It promotes hostility, mistrust, and violence, creating a hostile environment that hampers meaningful dialogue, cooperation, and consensus-building necessary for democratic governance. Furthermore, communal politics and vote bank strategies that exploit religious or ethnic sentiments can distort the democratic process. Such strategies prioritize sectarian interests over the broader welfare of society, compromising the principles of equal representation and the pursuit of the common good. To address the challenge of communalism in democracy, it is crucial to promote interfaith and intercultural dialogue, foster inclusive policies that protect minority rights, and actively work towards building a society based on equality, respect, and mutual understanding. Strong legal frameworks and institutions that protect against discrimination and promote social harmony are essential in countering the divisive impacts of communalism and safeguarding the democratic fabric of a nation.
- **Unemployment:** Firstly, unemployment creates economic hardships for individuals and households, resulting in inequality and social unrest. The lack of job opportunities and financial security can lead to frustration, disillusionment, and discontent among the unemployed, which may manifest in social and political tensions. Secondly, unemployment undermines the social fabric of a democratic society. It can lead to a sense of marginalization and exclusion, as individuals may feel disconnected from the benefits and opportunities of the democratic system. Unemployment can erode trust in institutions and contribute to social divisions, as people may perceive that the system is not adequately addressing their needs and concerns. Moreover, unemployment can impact political participation. When individuals are struggling to secure

employment or meet their basic needs, they may be less inclined to engage in political activities or exercise their democratic rights. This can lead to a decline in voter turnout, reduced citizen participation, and a sense of disengagement from the political process. To address the challenge of unemployment in democracy, it is essential to promote inclusive economic policies that stimulate job creation, encourage entrepreneurship, and foster sustainable economic growth. Investing in education, skills training, and social safety nets can help equip individuals with the tools they need to enter the workforce and mitigate the negative effects of unemployment. By addressing unemployment, democracies can ensure greater social cohesion, economic well-being, and active citizen participation, thereby strengthening the democratic system as a whole.

6

Independent Election Commission in India and It's Powers

The Election Commission of India is an independent constitutional body that has the responsibility of managing elections in India. It oversees the electoral processes for various positions such as the Lok Sabha, Rajya Sabha, state Legislative Assemblies, as well as the offices of the President and Vice President. The Election Commission operates under the authority of the Constitution, specifically Article 324, and the Representation of the People Act. In situations where existing laws are inadequate to handle specific election-related issues, the Commission has the power to take appropriate action in accordance with the Constitution.

In 1950, the Election Commission of India consisted of only a Chief Election Commissioner. However, on October 16, 1989, two additional Commissioners were appointed, albeit for a short period until January 1, 1990. The Election Commissioner Amendment Act of 1989 transformed the Commission into a multi-member body. Since then, a 3-member Commission has been in operation, with decisions being made through a majority vote.

The Chief Election Commissioner and the two Election Commissioners, who are typically retired IAS officers, receive salaries and allowances equivalent to those of Supreme Court judges, in accordance with the Chief Election Commissioner and other Election Commissioners (Conditions of Service) Rules, 1992. The Election Commission has a Secretariat located in New Delhi, which supports its functioning. The Election Commissioners receive assistance from Deputy Election Commissioners, usually IAS officers, as well as Directors General, Principal Secretaries, Secretaries, and Under Secretaries.

At the state level, the Election Commission is supported by the Chief Electoral Officer of the State, who holds the position of an IAS officer at the rank of Principal Secretary. The Chief Electoral Officer plays a crucial role in coordinating and overseeing the electoral process within the state.

At the district and constituency levels, the responsibilities for election-related tasks are carried out by the District Magistrates. They assume the roles of District Election Officers, Electoral Registration Officers, and Returning

Officers. These officers are responsible for organizing and conducting elections in their respective districts or constituencies. They handle tasks such as voter registration, polling station setup, voter education, and ensuring a smooth and fair election process.

The collective efforts of the Chief Electoral Officer, District Magistrates, and their respective teams contribute to the successful execution of elections at the state and local levels, ensuring the integrity and transparency of the electoral process.

Powers and Functions of Election Commission of India

- **Identification of constituencies:** The Commission is responsible for the delimitation or redrawing of electoral boundaries for parliamentary and assembly constituencies. The demarcation process aims to ensure equal representation by balancing population size, geographical considerations, and administrative convenience. It involves analyzing population data, taking into account factors such as population growth, demographic changes, and geographical features. The Election Commission reviews and revises constituency boundaries periodically to maintain a fair and equitable distribution of seats. This helps in addressing population shifts and changes in demographics, ensuring that each constituency has a comparable number of voters to maintain the principle of "one person, one vote." The demarcation process is conducted in consultation with various stakeholders, including political parties, local authorities, and members of the public. It involves gathering feedback, considering objections and suggestions, and making necessary adjustments to constituency boundaries based on the inputs received. The Election Commission's objective in demarcating constituencies is to achieve fair representation and ensure that every voter has an equal opportunity to participate in the democratic process. By ensuring a balanced distribution of constituencies, the Commission aims to uphold the democratic principle of effective and equitable representation of citizens in the legislative bodies.
- **Electoral Rolls:** Electoral rolls are an essential component of the electoral process, and the Election Commission of India holds the responsibility of preparing and maintaining these rolls. Electoral rolls, also known as voter lists or voter registers, are comprehensive databases that contain the names and other details of eligible voters in a particular constituency. The preparation of electoral rolls involves a systematic and meticulous process. The Election Commission conducts a door-to-door

enumeration or revision process to identify and register eligible voters. During this process, enumerators visit households to collect information such as names, addresses, age, and other relevant details of individuals who are eligible to vote. The collected data is then compiled, verified, and cross-checked to eliminate duplicates, errors, and ineligible entries. The Election Commission also undertakes efforts to include eligible citizens who may have been left out during the enumeration process, ensuring that the electoral rolls are as accurate and inclusive as possible. Electoral rolls play a crucial role in ensuring the integrity of the electoral process. They serve as the basis for determining the eligibility of individuals to vote in elections. Political parties, candidates, and election officials rely on electoral rolls to identify and communicate with voters, issue voter ID cards, and facilitate the smooth conduct of elections. The Election Commission regularly updates and maintains electoral rolls to reflect changes such as new registrations, change of address, and removal of deceased voters. It also provides opportunities for citizens to verify their details, make corrections, and raise objections if they believe there are inaccuracies in the rolls.

- **Recognition of Political Parties and Allotment of Symbols:** The Election Commission of India is responsible for the recognition of political parties and the allotment of symbols to these parties during elections. The recognition of a political party is essential for it to participate in the electoral process and avail certain benefits, such as access to electoral rolls, free airtime on state-run media, and reserved party symbols. To obtain recognition, political parties need to fulfill certain criteria set by the Election Commission. These criteria include having a minimum number of members, a registered office, and a commitment to uphold democratic principles. Parties are required to submit an application along with relevant documents to the Election Commission for consideration. Upon review of the application and compliance with the prescribed criteria, the Election Commission grants recognition to the political party. The recognition status allows the party to contest elections under its registered name, field candidates, and campaign for public support. Along with recognition, the Election Commission also allots unique symbols to political parties. These symbols play a significant role in distinguishing parties and candidates during elections, particularly in regions where there is a high illiteracy rate. Parties can choose from a list of free symbols, or if eligible, they can request a reserved symbol. The allotment of symbols is based on various factors, including the party's recognition status, past performance in elections, and the availability of symbols. The Election Commission ensures that symbols are allocated fairly and without bias to maintain a level playing field for all political parties. The recognition of political parties and the allotment of symbols by the Election Commission aim to promote transparency, prevent confusion among voters, and facilitate the democratic electoral process in India.

- **Scrutiny of the Nomination Papers:** The Election Commission examines the nomination papers submitted by candidates, accepting those that meet the required criteria and rejecting those that do not. The Returning Officer, responsible for this task, informs the candidates about the scheduled date, time, and venue for the formal scrutiny of nomination papers. During the scrutiny, the Returning Officer carefully reviews all the nomination papers, considering any objections raised. The officer ensures that the necessary requirements, such as the security deposit, election symbol, and election agent, have been fulfilled by the candidates. The scrutiny process is conducted with both efficiency and fairness, as the Returning Officer examines the papers and makes decisions accordingly.
- **The Conduct of the Poll:** The Election Commission is responsible for overseeing the entire polling process across India. In a Parliamentary or Assembly constituency, the Returning Officer, with the prior approval of the Election Commission, makes necessary arrangements for conducting the poll. In exceptional circumstances, the Commission has the authority to order a re-poll for the entire constituency. Article 324 of the Constitution grants the Election Commission the essential powers to conduct elections. This includes the power to countermand the poll in a constituency and order a fresh poll in cases where there is hooliganism, disruption of law and order, or other significant issues during polling or vote counting. These powers vested in the Election Commission ensure that the electoral process is conducted in a fair, free, and peaceful manner. The Commission can take decisive actions to address any circumstances that may jeopardize the integrity or smooth conduct of the election, thereby upholding the democratic principles and ensuring a level playing field for all candidates and voters.
- **Election Expenses:** One of the controversial functions of the Election Commission is to examine and scrutinize the accounts of election expenses submitted by candidates. In India, every candidate participating in an election is required to maintain and file their election expense accounts within a specified period after the election result is published.

The Returning Officer, within 10 days of the deadline for filing returns, provides the Election Commission with a list of all the candidates and their agents, along with their expense returns. The Returning Officer also includes observations regarding candidates who have failed to submit their returns within the specified time and in accordance with the prescribed procedure. The Election Commission carefully scrutinizes these accounts to determine if they are in the proper format and have been submitted within the designated timeframe. If any candidate or their agent fails to meet these requirements, the Election Commission notifies them of their disqualification by publishing the details in the official Gazette. This function is often controversial as it involves assessing the financial aspects of election campaigns and ensuring that candidates adhere to the established rules and regulations regarding election expenses. By scrutinizing the accounts, the Election Commission aims to maintain transparency, fairness, and accountability in the electoral process.

- **Advice to President:** The Election Commission holds the responsibility of advising the President or the Governor, as the case may be, on matters of disqualification of members of Parliament or State legislatures. Article 324 of the Constitution needs to be interpreted in conjunction with the constitutional framework and the Representation of the People Acts of 1950 and 1951. However, there are two limitations to the exercise of the Election Commission's plenary power. Firstly, if Parliament or any State legislature has enacted a valid law concerning elections, the Commission is obligated to act in accordance with that law. In cases where such a law does not provide specific guidance, Article 324 serves as a reservoir of power for the Commission to act in pursuit of conducting free and fair elections efficiently. Secondly, the Commission must adhere to the rule of law, act in good faith, and adhere to the principles of natural justice to the extent that such compliance can reasonably and realistically be expected of it. These limitations ensure that the Election Commission operates within the legal framework, respects the principles of fairness and justice, and upholds the purpose of conducting elections that are transparent, equitable, and efficient.
- **Conducting Elections:** The Election Commission is responsible for conducting elections to the Lok Sabha, Rajya Sabha, State Legislative Assemblies, and the offices of the President and Vice President of India. It prepares and maintains electoral rolls, sets up polling stations, and oversees the entire election process.

- **Voter Education and Awareness:** The Commission carries out extensive voter education and awareness programs to inform citizens about their rights, the importance of voting, and the electoral process. It aims to enhance voter participation and promote informed decision-making.
- **Settling Election Disputes:** The Commission has the authority to settle election disputes and complaints related to the conduct of elections. It adjudicates cases filed by candidates or political parties and ensures a fair resolution within the legal framework.

7

Local Self-Government Bodies

Local government is essential for responsive governance, citizen participation, effective service delivery, and sustainable development at the grassroots level. It ensures that decisions are made with the best interests of the community in mind, leading to improved quality of life and overall well-being for its residents. Local government ensures that decision-making is participatory, responsive, and tailored to the needs of the community, promoting effective governance and sustainable development at the grassroots level.

Importance of local government can be seen in the management of public parks and recreational facilities within a city. Local governments are responsible for maintaining and improving these spaces, ensuring that they are clean, safe, and accessible to the community. Through the local government's involvement, citizens can enjoy well-maintained parks with amenities such as playgrounds, walking trails, sports fields, and picnic areas. These spaces provide opportunities for recreation, exercise, and social interaction, contributing to the overall quality of life in the community. By taking an active role in managing public parks, local governments demonstrate their commitment to enhancing the community's well-being and promoting a sense of pride and ownership among residents. This example highlights the importance of local government in providing and maintaining essential public amenities that directly impact the daily lives and recreational opportunities of community members.

This chapter elaborates the role of local government at various levels both in the rural as well as urban areas.

Concept of Panchayati Raj

The concept of Panchayati Raj is rooted in both the ancient Indian belief that "God resides in the Panch" (the group of five) and the vision put forth by Mahatma Gandhi. Gandhi passionately advocated for power to be decentralized and accessible to all segments of society, emphasizing the significance of grassroots democracy. The realization of this vision relies on the establishment and empowerment of village panchayats.

The concept of Panchayati Raj is a system of local self-governance in India. It involves the establishment of elected village panchayats as the basic units of administration at the grassroots level. Panchayati Raj aims to decentralize power, promote participatory democracy, and address the specific needs of local communities. It provides an opportunity for citizens to actively participate in decision-making processes, fosters community development, and empowers rural areas by giving them control over their own governance and development initiatives.

Importance of Panchayati Raj

Until the British era, panchayats held significant importance in village social life and played a role in resolving minor disputes among villagers. However, during British rule, panchayats gradually lost their influence and authority due to the introduction of new court systems, laws, and revenue collection methods. Despite the Directive Principles of State Policy in India's Constitution after independence, which emphasized organizing village panchayats and granting them necessary powers for self-governance, Panchayati Raj was not given due attention by the states. Nevertheless, they have now been granted Constitutional recognition.

Structure of Government Recommended by the Balwant Rai Mehta Committee and the Ashok Mehta Committee

The Balwant Rai Mehta Committee, appointed in 1957, and the Ashok Mehta Committee, formed in 1977, made significant recommendations regarding the structure of government and the functioning of Panchayati Raj institutions in India.

The Balwant Rai Mehta Committee recommended the establishment of a three-tier Panchayati Raj system comprising village, block, and district levels. It emphasized the importance of democratic decentralization, empowering local bodies with political, administrative, and financial powers. The committee proposed direct elections, reservation of seats for marginalized groups, and devolution of functions, funds, and functionaries to ensure effective local governance.

The Ashok Mehta Committee, on the other hand, focused on strengthening Panchayati Raj institutions further. It suggested greater involvement of political parties, better coordination between Panchayati Raj bodies and other governmental agencies, and the creation of a separate ministry to oversee their functioning. The committee emphasized the need for financial autonomy, capacity building, and regular elections to promote the credibility and effectiveness of Panchayati Raj institutions.

Both committees aimed to enhance grassroots democracy, empower local communities, and ensure their active participation in decision-making processes. These recommendations have played a significant role in shaping the Panchayati Raj system in India and have guided subsequent reforms to strengthen local self-governance.

The three-tier Structure of Panchayati Raj

The three-tier structure of Panchayati Raj refers to the system of local self-government in India that consists of three levels of elected Panchayati Raj institutions at the grassroots level. These tiers are:

1. Panchayats at Village Level

This represents the foundational level of the Panchayati Raj system. The governing body for a village or a cluster of villages consists of two components: (i) Gram Sabha, which serves as a tangible representation of direct democracy, and (ii) Gram Panchayat.

(a) ***Gram Sabha:*** Gram Sabha is a key component of the Panchayati Raj system and represents direct democracy at the grassroots level. It serves as a forum where all the adults in a village or a group of villages come together to discuss and make decisions on various local issues. The Gram Sabha plays a vital role in promoting transparency, inclusivity, and community participation in the decision-making process of the Panchayat. Typically, there are six annual meetings of the Gram Sabha. During these meetings, the general body of villagers reviews financial statements, audit reports, and administrative updates from the Panchayats. Additionally, the Gram Sabha suggests new development initiatives for the Panchayats to undertake. It also assists in identifying individuals in need of economic support within the village, ensuring they receive appropriate assistance.

(b) ***Gram Panchayat:*** Gram Panchayat is the governing body at the village level in the Panchayati Raj system. It consists of elected representatives who are responsible for local governance and decision-making. The Gram Panchayat handles various administrative functions such as infrastructure development, welfare programs, public health, education, and agriculture. It plays a crucial role in implementing government schemes, resolving local disputes, and managing village resources. The Gram Panchayat serves as a vital link between the community and higher levels of government, working towards the overall development and well-being of the village and its residents. The members of a Gram Panchayat are directly elected by the villagers. The size of the Gram Panchayat is determined based on the population of the village, resulting in variation from one Panchayat to another. Elections are conducted through single-member constituencies. As mentioned earlier, one-third of the seats are reserved for women, as well as for Scheduled Castes and Tribes, with one-third specifically reserved for women belonging to Scheduled Castes and Tribes. The leaders of the Gram Panchayats are known by different names in different states, such as 'Sarpanch' or 'Pradhan'. There is also a Vice-Chairperson who is elected by the Panchayat members. The Gram Panchayats typically hold monthly meetings. Additionally, committees are formed at all levels of the Panchayati Raj system to facilitate the smooth functioning and management of their respective responsibilities.

2. Panchayat Samiti

Panchayat Samiti is an intermediary level of the Panchayati Raj system, situated above the Gram Panchayat but below the Zilla Parishad. It is responsible for overseeing a group of Gram Panchayats within a block or a taluka. The members of the Panchayat Samiti are elected by the people, with representation based on the population and area of the respective block. The Panchayat Samiti plays a vital role in coordinating and implementing developmental programs, providing public services, and addressing the needs of the villages under its jurisdiction. It also acts as a platform for the Gram Panchayats to voice their concerns and seek support for their initiatives. The Panchayat Samiti conducts regular meetings to discuss and decide on matters related to rural development, infrastructure, social welfare, and other administrative functions.

Within the Panchayat Samiti, a portion of its members are directly elected, specifically the Sarpanchs of Gram Panchayats. However, it's important to note that not all Sarpanchs simultaneously serve as members of the Panchayat Samiti. The number of Sarpanchs in the Panchayat Samiti varies from state to state and is rotated on an annual basis. Additionally, in some cases, members of Legislative Assemblies, Legislative Councils, and Parliament who belong to the Samiti area are co-opted as members of the Panchayat Samiti. Generally, the chairpersons of the Panchayat Samiti are elected from among the directly elected members.

3. Zila Parishad

Zila Parishad is the highest level of the Panchayati Raj system at the district level. It acts as the apex governing body responsible for overseeing and coordinating the development and administration of rural areas within the district. The members of the Zila Parishad are elected by the voters within the district. It is headed by a Chairperson and consists of elected representatives from various Panchayat Samitis within the district. The Zila Parishad plays a crucial role in planning and implementing development programs, allocating resources, and supervising the functioning of lower-level Panchayat institutions. It acts as a link between the state government and the grassroots-level Panchayats, ensuring effective governance, resource utilization, and equitable distribution of services at the district level. Zila Parishad holds monthly meetings to discuss various matters. Additionally, if there are specific issues or concerns that need to be addressed, special meetings can be arranged. Furthermore, subject committees are established to focus on specific areas of interest or expertise within the Zila Parishad.

In this framework, the panchayat samiti held the utmost significance. These three entities were interconnected, with the lower body being represented in the higher body through its chairperson. The Panchayati Raj system, following the pattern proposed by the Balwant Rai Mehta Committee, was initially implemented in Nagour of Rajasthan state on 2th October 1959. Subsequently, other states also adopted this model. During its early stages, both the people and the states showed great enthusiasm towards the implementation of Panchayati Raj.

The two-tier Structure

The government established the Ashok Mehta Committee with the purpose of examining Panchayati Raj, and its report was submitted in 1978. According to this committee, Panchayati Raj had succeeded in fostering political consciousness among rural communities. However, it had not effectively facilitated economic progress. Unlike the Balwant Rai Mehta Committee, the Ashok Mehta Committee proposed a two-tier structure for Panchayati Raj. These two tiers were envisioned as follows:

The two-tier structure of Panchayati Raj refers to a system where there are two levels of elected Panchayati Raj institutions at the local self-government level. This structure, recommended by the Ashok Mehta Committee, consists of the following tiers:

1. **Mandal Panchayat:** Mandal panchayat at the lower level, represents a group of villages. It is responsible for addressing local issues, implementing developmental programs, and ensuring community participation in decision-making.
2. **Zilla Parishad:** At the higher level, the Zilla Parishad represents the entire district and consists of representatives from various Gram Panchayats. It oversees the functioning of Gram Panchayats, coordinates

development activities at the district level, and manages district-level projects and programs.

The emphasis in the two-tier structure was on the zila parishad rather than the panchayat samiti, which differed from the previous committee report. Unfortunately, the Ashok Mehta Committee's recommendations could not be followed due to the Janata Government's demise in 1980. Some states, like Bihar, Uttar Pradesh, and Tamil Nadu, did not hold panchayat elections for an extended period of time. During this time, the Central Government established numerous new agencies, such as the District Rural Development Agency, to undertake collaborative development programs with the State Governments, but the panchayats were excluded from these initiatives. The panchayats themselves had limited financial resources to undertake development projects in the villages.

Formation of Panchayats

The Panchayati Raj system, established under the 73rd Amendment, is a three-tier structure where people directly elect representatives at the village, intermediate, and district levels. Small states with a population of less than 20 lakhs have the option to skip the intermediate level. All members of a Panchayat are directly elected, but some states may choose to include State Legislature and Parliament members in district and intermediate level Panchayats. The intermediate level Panchayats are commonly known as Panchayat Samitis. The chairpersons of village Panchayats are also included in block and district level Panchayats. Reservation of seats for Scheduled Castes and Scheduled Tribes, as well as one-third of seats for women, has been mentioned earlier. It's important to note that one-third of the reserved seats for women are specifically allotted to women from Scheduled Castes/Tribes. Seats for chairpersons are also reserved. The reserved seats are allocated through rotation among different constituencies within a Panchayat area. State Legislatures have the authority to provide further reservation for Other Backward Classes (OBC) in Panchayats.

The term of Panchayats refers to the duration for which elected representatives serve in their respective Panchayat positions. The duration varies based on the specific provisions of the governing legislation in different regions. Generally, the term of Panchayats is of five years. At the end of the term, fresh elections are conducted to elect new representatives. If a panchayat is dissolved earlier, elections are held within six months. This periodic election process ensures a continuous democratic functioning of the Panchayat institutions and allows for the rotation of leadership and representation at the grassroots level of governance.

Panchayats hold significant powers and responsibilities in local governance. They play a vital role in planning and implementing development projects, managing finances, providing public services, and resolving disputes at the grassroots level. Panchayats have the authority to govern and administer their respective areas, allocate resources, and promote social welfare. They empower local communities, encourage participation, and ensure democratic decision-making. They have the authority to create initiatives pertaining to 29 significant areas, including agriculture, primary and secondary education, healthcare, sanitation, access to clean water, rural housing, welfare of marginalized communities, social forestry, and more. These initiatives aim to promote economic development and social justice within their jurisdiction. With their focus on sustainable development and community needs, Panchayats foster inclusive governance and strive to enhance the overall well-being of the residents in their jurisdiction.

8

Urban Local Institutions

Urban local bodies refer to the local government institutions that are responsible for the administration and governance of urban areas. These bodies are established to address the specific needs and challenges of urban areas, including cities, towns, and other urban settlements. Urban local bodies play a crucial role in managing urban infrastructure, providing essential services, and promoting urban development. They are responsible for areas such as urban planning, public health, sanitation, solid waste management, transportation, water supply, and housing. The composition and structure of urban local bodies vary across different countries and regions, but they typically consist of elected representatives who work towards the overall development and well-being of urban communities.

There are three types of urban local bodies: Municipal Corporations for large cities, Municipal Councils for smaller cities, and Nagar Panchayats for areas that are transitioning from rural to urban. Unlike Panchayati Raj Institutions (PRIs), urban local bodies are independent and not closely connected to each other. In a single state, you can find all three types of urban local bodies, such as a Municipal Corporation in a big city, a Municipal Council in a smaller city, and a Nagar Panchayat in a small town. The first urban local government was established in Madras (now Chennai) in 1688 during British colonial rule, followed by similar bodies in Kolkata and Mumbai. These municipalities were initially formed to improve sanitation and prevent epidemics. The 74th Constitutional Amendment in 1992 brought significant changes to the urban local government system, and now Municipal Corporations, Municipal Councils, and Nagar Panchayats operate as different types of urban local bodies.

Recommended changes as per the 74th Constitutional Amendment 1992

The 74th Constitutional Amendment Act of 1992 introduced substantial changes to the structure and functioning of urban local government. Here are some important points to note:

1. Each Indian state must establish urban local bodies, which include Municipal Corporations, Municipal Councils, and Nagar Panchayats.

2. Wards Committees should be formed within the municipal area to ensure people's participation in local civic matters at the grassroots level.
3. State Election Commissions are responsible for conducting municipal elections in a regular and fair manner.
4. In cases where necessary, municipal governments may be temporarily suspended for a maximum period of six months.
5. Municipal governments must ensure adequate representation of weaker sections of society (such as Scheduled Castes, Scheduled Tribes, and Backward Classes) and women through reserved seats.
6. The State Legislatures have the authority to specify the powers and functional responsibilities, including financial matters, to be entrusted to municipalities and wards committees through legislation.
7. State Finance Commissions are established every five years to assess the financial status of municipalities and make recommendations for improving their financial position.
8. District Planning Committees at the district level and Metropolitan Planning Committees in metropolitan areas of each state are formed to prepare and consolidate development plans.

1. Municipal Corporations (Mahanagar Palika / Nagar Nigam)

Municipal Corporations have significant powers and responsibilities in managing the affairs of the city. They play a crucial role in urban planning, infrastructure development, public health, sanitation, water supply, waste management, and other essential services. They are responsible for maintaining public facilities, such as roads, parks, and public buildings, and promoting the overall well-being and development of the city.

The Municipal Corporation is headed by an elected Mayor or Commissioner who serves as the chief executive and also known as first citizen of the city. The Corporation consists of elected representatives, known as Councillors, who represent various wards within the city. The Councillors of Municipal Corporations are elected for 5 years. The elected Councillors elect one of them as Mayor annually. These representatives participate in decision-making processes, budget allocation, and policy formulation to address the needs and aspirations of the residents.

Municipal Corporations provide a platform for local governance, citizen engagement, and community participation. They serve as the voice of the people, advocating for their interests, and implementing initiatives to enhance the quality of life in the urban areas they govern.

Through their authority and resources, Municipal Corporations have the potential to shape and transform cities, making them more livable, sustainable, and inclusive. They play a vital role in managing the rapid urbanization and addressing the challenges faced by urban areas, ultimately contributing to the overall development and growth of the city and its inhabitants.

Reserved seats are allocated for Scheduled Castes, Scheduled Tribes, and other marginalized sections in proportion to their population. Among the reserved seats for Scheduled Castes and Scheduled Tribes, one-third is specifically reserved for women from these communities. If a Municipal Corporation is dissolved, elections must be held within six months. The Municipal Commissioner, who serves as the Chief Executive Officer, is an official appointed by the State government. In the case of Union Territories like Delhi, this appointment is made by the Central government.

Functions of the Municipal Corporations

Municipal Corporations have various functions and responsibilities to ensure the effective administration and development of the cities they govern. These functions ensure that Municipal Corporations effectively address the needs and aspirations of the city's residents and contribute to the overall development and well-being of the urban area. Some of the key functions of Municipal Corporations include:

1. ***Urban Planning:*** Municipal Corporations are responsible for urban planning and development, including land use regulations, zoning, and infrastructure development.
2. ***Public Health and Sanitation:*** They play a vital role in maintaining public health and sanitation standards within the city. This includes waste management, sanitation services, and ensuring a clean and healthy environment.
3. ***Infrastructure Development:*** Municipal Corporations are involved in the development and maintenance of essential urban infrastructure, such as roads, bridges, street lighting, parks, and public transportation.
4. ***Water Supply and Sewerage:*** They ensure a reliable supply of clean drinking water to residents and manage the city's sewerage and drainage systems.
5. ***Public Services:*** Municipal Corporations provide various public services, including healthcare facilities, education, libraries, recreational facilities, and cultural programs.

6. ***Licensing and Regulation:*** They regulate and issue licenses for commercial activities, trade, and establishments, ensuring compliance with relevant laws and regulations.
7. ***Revenue Generation:*** Municipal Corporations collect taxes, fees, and charges from residents and businesses to generate revenue for funding public services and infrastructure development.
8. ***Social Welfare:*** They implement welfare schemes and programs for the welfare of marginalized sections, such as Scheduled Castes, Scheduled Tribes, and economically weaker sections of society.
9. ***Disaster Management:*** Municipal Corporations play a crucial role in disaster preparedness, response, and recovery in case of natural disasters or emergencies.
10. ***Community Engagement:*** They encourage citizen participation and engagement through forums, public consultations, and community development initiatives to address local issues and promote civic involvement.

2. Municipal Councils (Municipality/ Nagar Palika)

Municipal Councils are an integral part of the urban local government system in India. They are one of the three types of urban local bodies, alongside Municipal Corporations and Nagar Panchayats. Municipal Councils are responsible for governing and managing smaller cities and towns in the country. Municipal Councils are established to ensure local self-governance and provide efficient administration at the grassroots level. They play a crucial role in addressing the needs and concerns of residents in smaller urban areas and promoting their overall development.

Elections for Municipal Councils are conducted by the State Election Commissions on a regular basis. The electoral process allows citizens to participate in the selection of their local representatives who will work towards the betterment of their respective municipalities. During the elections, eligible voters cast their votes to elect councilors for five years who will represent their respective wards within the municipality. These councilors play an essential role in decision-making, policy formulation, and allocation of resources for the development and welfare of their communities.

The election process ensures that the Municipal Councils reflect the diversity and aspirations of the local population. It provides an opportunity for citizens to voice their concerns and elect representatives who can effectively address their needs, advocate for their interests, and work towards the overall progress of their respective municipalities.

Municipal Councils, through their elected representatives, serve as a crucial link between the local government and the residents. They play a pivotal role in urban planning, infrastructure development, provision of basic services, and addressing local issues to enhance the quality of life for the citizens.

Functions of the Municipal Council

Municipal Councils have various functions and responsibilities similar to municipal corporation, aimed at effective governance and development of the cities and towns they govern. Some of the key functions of Municipal Councils include:

1. ***Urban Planning:*** Municipal Councils play a vital role in urban planning, including land use management, development control, and ensuring adherence to building regulations and zoning laws.
2. ***Infrastructure Development:*** They are responsible for the development and maintenance of urban infrastructure such as roads, bridges, street lighting, public transportation systems, and parks.
3. ***Water Supply and Sanitation:*** Municipal Councils ensure a reliable supply of clean drinking water to residents and manage the sanitation and waste management systems in the municipality.
4. ***Public Health and Sanitation:*** They are responsible for maintaining public health standards, including sanitation services, waste disposal, and disease control measures within the municipality.
5. ***Civic Amenities:*** Municipal Councils provide and maintain civic amenities such as public toilets, community halls, libraries, sports facilities, and recreational spaces for the residents.
6. ***Licensing and Regulation:*** They regulate and issue licenses for various activities, including commercial establishments, trade licenses, and permissions for events and gatherings.
7. ***Taxation and Revenue Generation:*** Municipal Councils levy and collect taxes, fees, and charges from residents and businesses to generate revenue for funding public services and infrastructure development.
8. ***Social Welfare:*** They implement welfare schemes and programs for the benefit of marginalized sections of society, including economically weaker sections and disadvantaged communities.
9. ***Public Services:*** Municipal Councils provide essential public services such as healthcare facilities, primary education, street maintenance, street lighting, and public transportation.

10. ***Community Development:*** They engage in community development initiatives, promote citizen participation, and encourage local participation in decision-making processes through public consultations, citizen forums, and awareness campaigns.

3. Nagar Panchayats

Nagar Panchayats are established to ensure effective local self-governance and provide basic civic amenities and services to the residents of semi-urban areas (more than 30,000 and less than 100,000 inhabitants). They serve as an important administrative unit, bridging the gap between rural and urban areas and addressing the unique challenges faced by these transitional regions. These local bodies aim to promote the overall development and welfare of the semi-urban areas under their jurisdiction. They play a significant role in the planning and implementation of infrastructure projects, public services, and social welfare programs tailored to meet the specific needs of the semi-urban population.

Nagar Panchayats have limited jurisdiction compared to Municipal Corporations and Municipal Councils, focusing primarily on basic services such as water supply, sanitation, street lighting, public health, and primary education. As semi-urban areas continue to evolve and grow, the role of Nagar Panchayats becomes increasingly important in facilitating their transition into fully urbanized areas.

The creation and functioning of Nagar Panchayats are guided by relevant state legislation and regulations. They are typically administered by a council consisting of elected representatives who work towards the development and improvement of the semi-urban areas in consultation with the local community. Nagar Panchayats provide an essential governance structure for semi-urban areas, allowing residents to actively participate in decision-making processes and ensuring that their specific needs are addressed. These local bodies serve as a critical link between rural and urban development, fostering inclusive growth and providing a platform for local concerns and aspirations to be heard and acted upon.

9

Rural Local Institutions

The Balwant Rai Mehta Committee, in its 1957 report, proposed the establishment of a Panchayati Raj System consisting of three tiers: Gram Panchayats at the village level, Panchayat Samitis at the block or intermediate level, and Zila Parishad at the district level. The National Development Council also supported a similar structure in 1958, with villages at the bottom and districts at the top. However, it was the 73rd Constitutional Amendment in 1992 that gave the Panchayati Raj System its current form. Most states now have Panchayati Raj Institutions operating at three levels: village, intermediate, and district. However, smaller states with populations under 20 lakh have only two tiers: the village level and the district level. These institutions have various functions and responsibilities, such as infrastructure development, social welfare initiatives, provision of basic services, rural development planning, promoting grassroots democracy, etc. They also facilitate the participation of marginalized sections of society, including Scheduled Castes, Scheduled Tribes, and women, through reserved seats and representation. This chapters explores duties and functions of rural institutions given below;

Functions/ Duties of Rural Institutions

1. Zila Parishad

Zila Parishad, which is the highest tier of Panchayati Raj Institutions at the district level, has several duties and functions. Some of the key duties and functions of Zila Parishad include:

1. ***Planning and Development:*** Zila Parishad plays a crucial role in the planning and implementation of development programs and projects at the district level. It prepares and approves the district-level plans, identifies priority areas for development, and allocates resources for various development schemes.
2. ***Resource Mobilization:*** Zila Parishad is responsible for mobilizing financial resources for local development initiatives. It explores funding opportunities from central and state governments, facilitates collaborations with non-governmental organizations and other stake-holders, and seeks external funding sources for district-level projects.

3. ***Infrastructure Development:*** Zila Parishad oversees the planning, implementation, and maintenance of infrastructure projects in the district. This includes the construction and maintenance of roads, bridges, schools, healthcare centers, water supply systems, and other public facilities required for the development and well-being of the district's population.
4. ***Service Delivery:*** Zila Parishad ensures the effective delivery of essential services to the district's residents. It monitors and supervises the functioning of primary healthcare centers, educational institutions, and other service providers in collaboration with relevant departments and agencies. It also works towards improving service quality and accessibility in the district.
5. ***Health facilities:*** Starting Primary Health Centers and hospitals in villages, managing mobile hospitals for hamlets, conducting vaccination drives against epidemics and family welfare campaigns.
6. ***Social Welfare:*** Zila Parishad focuses on the welfare of disadvantaged and marginalized sections of society. It implements social welfare programs, such as poverty alleviation initiatives, skill development programs, and social security schemes, to uplift the socio-economic conditions of vulnerable communities in the district.
7. ***Agri*cultural development:** Supplying improved seeds to farmers, informing them of new techniques of farming, undertaking construction of small-scale irrigation projects and percolation tanks, and maintaining pastures and grazing lands.
8. ***Natural Resource Management:*** Zila Parishad promotes sustainable management of natural resources within the district. It oversees activities related to watershed management, soil conservation, forest preservation, and other environmental conservation efforts. It works towards creating awareness about environmental issues and encourages eco-friendly practices.
9. ***Financial Management:*** Zila Parishad manages its own finances and resources. It prepares budgets, collects local taxes, levies, and user charges, and utilizes the funds for district-level development projects and welfare activities. It ensures transparency and accountability in financial management.
10. ***Coordination and Monitoring:*** Zila Parishad acts as a coordinating body among various government departments, local bodies, and agencies operating within the district. It ensures effective coordination

and collaboration among stakeholders for the successful implementation of development programs. It also monitors the progress and impact of projects and programs in the district.

11. ***Grievance Redressal:*** Zila Parishad provides a platform for addressing grievances and complaints from the residents of the district. It establishes mechanisms for receiving, investigating, and resolving grievances related to local governance, service delivery, and other district-level issues.

2. Panchayat Samiti

A Panchayat Samiti is a local government body that exists at the intermediate level between the village Panchayats and the district administration in India. It is a representative body responsible for the administration of rural areas within a specified jurisdiction. The members of a Panchayat Samiti are elected by the people through periodic elections. The elected representatives, known as Panchayat Samiti members, represent different constituencies within the Samiti's jurisdiction. They work collectively to address the needs and concerns of the local communities they represent.

Panchayat Samitis play a significant role in empowering rural communities, fostering participatory decision-making, and promoting socio-economic development in rural areas. They serve as a platform for democratic governance and help in ensuring the overall welfare and progress of the rural population in India. The Panchayat Samiti in India has several important duties and functions. Here are some of the key responsibilities they undertake:

1. ***Development Planning:*** Panchayat Samitis play a crucial role in planning and implementing development schemes and programs at the intermediate level. They identify the developmental needs of the rural areas within their jurisdiction and prepare plans for addressing those needs.
2. ***Infrastructure Development:*** Panchayat Samitis are responsible for the development and maintenance of basic rural infrastructure, including roads, bridges, water supply systems, sanitation facilities, and other essential amenities.
3. ***Service Delivery:*** They ensure the delivery of essential services such as primary healthcare, education, agriculture extension services, and social welfare programs to the rural population. Panchayat Samitis collaborate with relevant government departments and agencies to ensure efficient service delivery.

4. ***Resource Mobilization:*** Panchayat Samitis are authorized to collect local taxes, fees, and other revenues to generate funds for local development activities. They also receive funds from the central and state governments for implementing various developmental programs.
5. ***Coordination and Monitoring:*** Panchayat Samitis act as a coordinating body between the district administration and the village Panchayats. They monitor the functioning of the village Panchayats within their jurisdiction, provide guidance and support, and ensure compliance with rules and regulations.
6. ***Social Welfare:*** Panchayat Samitis work towards promoting social welfare and addressing the needs of marginalized communities. They implement poverty alleviation programs, welfare schemes for women, children, and senior citizens, and initiatives for the upliftment of backward classes.
7. ***Conflict Resolution:*** Panchayat Samitis facilitate the resolution of disputes and conflicts arising within their jurisdiction. They provide a platform for mediation and arbitration, helping to maintain peace and harmony in the rural areas.
8. ***Representation and Advocacy:*** Panchayat Samiti members represent the interests and concerns of their respective constituencies. They act as a voice for the local communities, advocating for their needs and rights at the higher levels of governance.

3. Gram Panchayat

A Gram Panchayat is the basic unit of local self-government in rural areas of India. It is the smallest administrative unit within the Panchayati Raj system and represents a group of villages. The term "Gram" refers to a village, and "Panchayat" means an assembly of elected representatives.

The key functions of a Gram Panchayat include providing basic civic amenities. Gram Panchayat also plays a crucial role in the implementation of various government schemes and programs aimed at rural development. It acts as a conduit for the delivery of essential services mentioned below:

1. ***Local Governance:*** The Gram Panchayat serves as the primary unit of local self-government in rural areas. Its primary duty is to govern the village or group of villages under its jurisdiction, making decisions on matters related to local development, administration, and welfare.
2. ***Infrastructure Development:*** The Gram Panchayat is responsible for the development and maintenance of local infrastructure. This includes the

construction and maintenance of roads, bridges, water supply systems, street lighting, public facilities, and other essential amenities within the village.

3. ***Public Services:*** The Gram Panchayat ensures the delivery of basic public services to the villagers. This includes providing access to education by managing local schools, promoting healthcare services, maintaining public health centers or dispensaries, and implementing sanitation programs.
4. ***Social Welfare:*** Gram Panchayats work towards the welfare of the rural population. They implement various social welfare programs and initiatives aimed at poverty alleviation, women's empowerment, child welfare, senior citizen support, and the upliftment of marginalized sections of society.
5. ***Resource Management:*** The Gram Panchayat manages and utilizes local resources for the benefit of the community. They mobilize funds through local taxes, grants, and central or state government schemes to finance local development projects and initiatives.
6. ***Village Planning and Development:*** Gram Panchayats are responsible for planning and executing village-level development programs. They identify the needs and priorities of the village and formulate plans for socio-economic development, environmental conservation, and sustainable growth.
7. ***Dispute Resolution:*** Gram Panchayats act as a platform for resolving disputes and conflicts within the village. They mediate and settle disputes relating to land, property, public amenities, and other local issues through a participatory and community-driven approach.
8. ***Public Awareness and Participation:*** Gram Panchayats promote awareness among the villagers about government programs, policies, and their rights. They encourage active participation and engagement of the community in local decision-making processes, fostering a sense of ownership and empowerment.

10

Constitutional Provision of 73rd & 74th Constitutional Amendment Act

Village Panchayats existed in India long back, but the system has inherent weaknesses like the inability to be a people's government responsiveness to their needs. This was due to a variety of factors like a lack of financial resources, no regular elections and inadequate representation of the weaker sections (scheduled castes/ tribes and women) of the society. The Directive Principles of State Policy in the Constitution of India lays down in Article 40 that the government should facilitate the establishment and smooth functioning of the gram panchayats.

To address these issues and strengthening the local self-government in India, the central government brought about the73rd Amendment Act in 1992. The Bill was passed by the Parliament on December 22, 1992 and is now known as the Constitution 73rd Amendment Act, 1992. The constituted 73rd Amendment Act, 1992 came into effect from 24th April 1993. The basic objective of the democratic decentralization through reactivation of the Panchayati Raj system was to realize Gandhiji's concept of "Swarajya".

The revitalization of Panchayati Raj manifested through the 73rd Constitution Amendment owes its origin to the dynamic leadership of Rajiv Gandhi. Panchayati Raj emerges as major institutional channel of such administration.

This Act added a new chapter into the constitution called 'Part IX: The Panchayatas'

The 73rd amendment brought the Panchayati raj System to rural India, the 74th Amendment brought the Municipality system to urban India. The 73rd and 74th Establishment of local self government bodies at rural and urban level there are separate provision of 73rd and 74th constitutional amendment Act in the Indian constitution.

Features of 73rd Constitutional Amendment Act

The passage of the Constitution (73rd Amendment) Act, 1992 marks a new era in the federal democratic set up of the country and provides constitutional status to the Panchayati Raj Institutions (PRIs). The chief features of the act are mentioned below:

1. The act made the Panchayati Raj Institutions in the country constitutional bodies.
2. Under Article 243-B, it has become compulsory for every state to establish panchayats in their territories.
3. It led to the establishment of a three-tier structure: Village Panchayat (Gram Panchayat); intermediate panchayat (Panchayat Samiti; and the district panchayat (Zila Parishad).
4. Article 243-G makes it mandatory for the state governments to develop powers, responsibilities and authority to the panchayats.
5. The gram panchayats have a fixed tenure of 5 years
6. Regular election every five years and the State election commissions have been provided with the mechanism to conduct independent elections to the village panchayats.
7. Provision was given in Article 243-D for the due representation of women and SC/St. There is reservation of seats for the scheduled tribes and scheduled castes in proportion to their population.
8. Establishment of State Finance Commissions to recommend measures to improve the finances and evaluate financial positions of Panchayats every five years.
9. Establishment of District Planning Committee to prepare development plans for the districts.
10. Preparation of plans for economic development and social justice and their execution concerning 29 subjects listed in the 11th Schedule of the Constitution
11. Establishment of Grama Sabha (village assemblies) and their empowerment as a decision making body at the village level
12. Rotation in accordance with the reservation of seats for women and the Scheduled Castes in the PRIs.

The passing of the 73rd Amendment has improved local self-government in the country vastly. By the Constitution (73rd Amendment) Act, the Panchayati Raj Institutions have been given such powers and authority as may be necessary to enable them to function. It contains provisions for devolution of powers and responsibilities related to (a) the preparation of plans for economic development and social justice; and (b) the implementation of such schemes for economic development and social justice as may be entrusted to them.

Upon the enactment of the 73rd Constitutional Amendment Act, almost all the States/UTs, have enacted their legislation. Moreover, almost all the States/

UTs have held local body elections. As a result, 255326 Panchayats at village level; 697 Panchayats at intermediate level and 665 Panchayats at district level have been constituted in the country. These Panchayats are being manned by about 29.2 lakh elected representatives of Panchayats at all levels. This is the broadest representative base that exists in any country of the world.

In order to celebrate this and further give impetus to the institutions, the central government in 2010 decided to observe 24th April every year as **National Panchayati Raj Day**.

The Constitution (74th Amendment) Act, 1992

The 74th Constitutional Amendment Act was passed to constitutionalise the system of Urban Local Government, also known as the Municipalities. The recommendations and suggestions of several commissions and committees appointed by the Central Government, from time to time, to improve the urban bodies resulted in the enactment of the Constitution (Seventy-fourth Amendment) Act, 1992.

The weakened status of Urban Local Bodies crystallized public opinion in favour of need for a Constitutional guarantee to safeguard the interests of urban local bodies in order to provide for

- Regular and fair conduct of elections to these bodies
- Holding of elections within a specified time limit in case of supersession
- Adequate representation of SC/ST and women in the elected bodies
- Placing on firm footing the relationship between the State Governments and the urban local bodies with respect to:
  - functions and taxation powers of the urban local bodies
  - arrangement for revenue sharing between the State Government and the urban local bodies.
- Involvement of elected representatives at grassroots level in planning at the district and metropolitan levels.

Earlier, State Governments were free to manage their local bodies as they wished. The Amendment made statutory provisions for the establishment, empowerment and functioning of urban local self-governing institutions. It provides a framework for the decentralization of obligations and duties to the Municipal bodies at different levels of a state. With the introduction of this act, an institutional framework was created to focus on the grassroots level and ensure efficient administration of urban areas through self-governing urban local bodies.

With this act that the urban local body, Municipalities, came under the purview of the provisions mentioned under the Indian Constitution. The main aim was to strengthen and revitalize the urban local bodies so that development can occur at all the levels of the nation.

The Amendment Act added a new part to the Constitution, Part IX-A, which consisted of Articles from 243-P to 243-ZG ensuring uniformity in the laws made for the municipalities.

The main provisions of this Act can be grouped under two categories– compulsory and voluntary. Some of the compulsory provisions which are binding on all States are:

1. Constitution of three types of municipalities depending upon size and area namely (i) Nagar Panchayat for an area in transition from rural to urban area; (ii) Municipal Councils for smaller urban area; and (iii) Municipal Corporations for larger urban area.
2. Constitution of Ward Committees in all municipalities with a population of 3 lakhs or more.
3. Reservation of seats in urban local bodies for Scheduled Castes / Scheduled Tribes roughly in proportion to their population. The reservation would be made in respect of seats to be filled by direct elections only.
4. Reservation of seats for women up to one-third seats;
5. The State Election Commission, constituted in order to conduct elections in the Panchayati Raj bodies (see 73rd Amendment) will also conduct elections to the urban local self- governing bodies;
6. The State Finance Commission, constituted under Article 243-I to deal with financial affairs of the Panchayati Raj bodies also looks into the financial affairs of the local urban self governing bodies and will make recommendations to the Governor.
7. Tenure of urban local self-governing bodies is fixed at five years and in case of earlier dissolution fresh elections are held within six months;
8. Planning and allocation of resources at the district level for the Panchayati Raj institutions are normally to be done by the Zilla Parishad. With regard to urban areas, municipal bodies discharge these functions within their respective jurisdictions

Some of the Voluntary Provisions which are not Binding, but are Expected to be Observed by the States are

a) Giving voting rights to members of the Union and State Legislatures in these bodies;

b) Providing reservation for backward classes;

c) Giving financial powers in relation to taxes, duties, tolls and fees, etc;

d) Making the municipal bodies autonomous and devolution of powers to these bodies to perform some or all of the functions enumerated in the Twelfth Schedule added to the Constitution through this Act and/or to prepare plans for economic development.

11

Important Features of 73rd and 74th Constitutional Amendment Act

The 73rd and the 74th Constitutional Amendment Acts, 1992 enjoin upon the states to establish a three-tier system of Panchayats at the village, intermediate and district levels and Municipalities in the urban areas respectively. States are expected to devolve adequate powers, responsibilities and finances upon these bodies so as to enable them to prepare plans and implement schemes for economic development and social justice.

These Acts provide a basic framework of decentralisation of powers and authorities to the Panchayati Raj/Municipal bodies at different levels.

The 73rd and the 74th Amendments to the Constitution of India are the new chapters in the democratic decentralization process in India.

The Salient Features of the 73rd Constitution Amendment Act are given below

The Amendment stipulates for certain compulsory provisions which are obligatory on the part of the State Governments to incorporate in their respective Acts. Some aspects have, however, been left at the discretion of State legislatures to make suitable provisions in their Act.

The mandatory provisions are:

1. Establishment of 'Gram Sabha' at the village level comprising of persons registered in the electoral rolls relating to a village comprised within the area of Panchayat (Article 243(b)). The State, where Gram Sabha does not exist, will have to make such provision.
2. Establishment of a three-tier system of Panchayat, at the village, intermediate and district levels, in all the States and Union Territories (UTs) except in those having a population of less than twenty lakhs where Panchayats at intermediate level need not be constituted. The States which will fall under this category as per 1991 census are Goa, Sikkim, all the North Eastern States and UTs.

3. All levels of Panchayats will consist of persons elected directly from the territorial constituencies in the Panchayat area. The territorial constituencies shall be carved out in such manner that the ratio between the population of each constituency and the number of seats allotted to it should be uniform throughout the Panchayat area as far as practicable.
4. All members of the Panchayat whether or not directly elected shall have the right to vote in the meetings of the Panchayats.
5. The chairperson of a Panchayat at the intermediate and district level shall bre elected from among the directly elected members representing the territorial constituencies.
6. Reservation of seats for SCs/STs in proportion to their population in the Panchayat area and seats may be allotted by rotation.
7. One-third of the total number of seats, both in reserved and unreserved categories shall be apart for women in every Panchayat and seats may be allotted by rotation.
8. The chairperson of each level of Panchayats shall be reserved for SCs/ STs in proportion to their population on rotation basis. Similarly, one-third post of chairpersons of each level of Panchayats shall be reserved for women on rotation basis.
9. A fixed tenure of five years for Panchayats from the data appointed for its first meeting and the tenure cannot be extended. However, if a Panchayat is dissolved before the expiry of its term, election is to conducted within a period of six months of the dissolution to reconstitute the Panchayat for the remainder of the terms of the term provided the remainder of the period is not less than six months. The Panchayats shall be constituted before the expiry of its tenure of five years.
10. Amendment of law to dissolve the Panchayats at any level is also prohibited.
11. A person who has attained twenty one years of age is eligible for a membership of a Panchayat.
12. Constitution of a Finance Commissiom in the State within one year from the commencement of the Constitution Amendment Act initially and thereafter every five years to review the finances of the Panchayats and recommended the principles on the basis of which the taxes to be appropriated by, or assigned to the Panchayats as also grant-in-aid to the Panchayats from the consolidated fund of the State. The action taken on the recommendation of the Commission shall be laid before the Legislature of the State.

13. Audit of the accounts of the Panchayats to be done.
14. A State Election Commission has to be constituted for the superintendence, direction and control of the Panchayats at all levels. The State Election Commissioner, however, shall be removed in the manner and on the like grounds as a Judge of a High Court.
15. The Act is applicable to all States and Union Territories. Exemption is being ranted to certain states and tribal areas and other territories from the application of the provisions of part IX of the Constitution and powers to the President and the Governor to modify the provisions of the IX in their application to Union Territories and Scheduled areas, respectively.
16. The existing laws relating to Panchyats which are inconsistent with the provision of the Act shall continue to be inforced until it is amended or repealed within one year. The existing Panchayats shall continue till the expiration of their terms unless they are dissolved by the competent authority.
17. Courts are not to interface in the electoral matters such as delimitation of constituencies, allotment of seats and election to any Panchayat. Petition challenging the election of any Panchayat can be presented to Besides these mandatory provisions the State Legislature has been empowered to have legislation in respect of a wide range of subjects, including on such matters as functions of the Panchayats and so on.

74th Amendment Act 1992 in India

The constitution 74th Amendment Act 1992, relating to Municipalities (Urban local Government) was passed by the parliament in 1992.

It received the assent of the president of India on 20th April 1993. The Act seeks to provide a common framework for the structure and mandate of urban local bodies to enable them to function as effective democratic units of local Self Government.

Government of India notified 1st June 1993 as the date from which the 74th Amendment Act came into force. The Act provided for a period of one year from the date of its commencement, within which the then existing municipal laws (which were in force at that time In states/union territories) were required to be changed/amended/modified in order to bring them in conformity with the provisions of the constitution (74th Amendment) Act—1992.

Some of the Provisions which are not Binding on the States, but only Guidelines are

a) Giving voting rights to members of the Central and State legislatures in these bodies;

b) Providing reservation for backward classes; and

c) The Panchayati Raj institutions should be given financial powers in relation to taxes, levy fees etc. and efforts shall be made to make Panchayats autonomous bodies.

Salient Features of 74th Constitutional Amendment Act

1. Constitution of urban local bodies (namely, ***Municipal Corporation, Municipal Council***, and ***Nagar Panchayat***) in every Indian State;
2. Constitution of **Wards Committees** within the territorial area of a municipality, to ensure people's participation in civic affairs at the grass-root level;
3. Regular and fair conduct of **municipal elections** by State Election Commissions;
4. Provision for supersession of municipal governments for not more than 6 months;
5. Adequate representation of weaker sections (i.e., Scheduled Castes, Scheduled Tribes, Backward Classes) of the society and women in municipal governments through **reservation** of seats;
6. Specification by law, through the State Legislatures, of the **powers** (including financial) and **functional responsibilities** to be entrusted to municipalities and wards committees;
7. Constitution of **State Finance Commissions**, once in every 5 years, to review the financial position of municipalities and to make recommendations on the measures needed to improve their financial position; and
8. Constitution of a **District Planning Committee** at the district level and a **Metropolitan Planning Committee** in metropolitan areas of every State, for the preparation and consolidation of development plans.

Difference between 73rd and 74th Amendments Act

73rd Amendment Act	74th Amendment Act
It brought the Panchayati Raj System to rural India.	It brought the Municipality System to urban India
It laid down a three-tier system that shall comprise to be the Panchayati Raj.	It gives provisions for estabilishing three types of municipalities in every state-Nagar panchayat, municipal council, and municipal corporation.
This made the Gram Sabha the fundamental basis of the Pancahayat Raj System to perform the duties and responsibilities assigned by the State governments.	The President of India assented to this act on 20 April 1993.
The amendment provides for a three-tier Panchayat Raj system at the Village, intermediate, and district levels.	It came into force on 1 June 1993
It added Part IX to the Indian Constitution	It added part IX- A to the Indian Constitution.
It contains article 243 to 234-O	It contains Article 243P -243 ZG

12

Good Governance

In recent years the terms "governance" and "good governance" are being used frequently in development literature. The concept of good governance is related to all branches of social sciences, especially, to political science, public administration, and economics. The term governance has become synonymous to sound development management. The concept of "governance" not new, it is as old as government itself. The term governance has become synonymous to sound development management. In recent times the concept of Good Governance first emerged in the mid-1980s as governability with the emphasis on adherence to the rule of law.

Origin of the Concept of Governance

This word is derived from the Greek word Kubernaein means to steer. Literally it means to 'control, guide or manipulate'. Simply governance means the process of decision making and the process by which decisions are implemented (or not implemented). Governance encompasses the system by which an organization is controlled and operates, and the mechanism by which it, and its people, are held to account.

During 1980s under economic reforms especially under globalization the use of term governance became popular with its emphasis on the process and manner of governing to the notion of sustainable development.

Meanwhile, organization such as IMF, NGOs, the UN and its agencies, the World Bank and international media were quick to pick up the term and use it in a variety of ways. Together with its derived term, good governance, the catch-all term governance has since become a buzzword in the vocabulary of polity and administrative reform in developing countries dependent on support from international development agencies.

Meaning

In 1989 World Bank study "Sub-Saharan Africa-from Crisis to Sustainable Growth", the term 'Governance' was first used to describe the need for institutional reform and a better and more efficient public sector in Sub-Saharan countries. It defined governance as "the exercise of political power to manage a nation's affairs."

However, it does not define word “good”. Later, the former World Bank president barber Conable (1986-1991) used the term ‘good governance’, which referred to as a ‘public service that is efficient, a judicial system that is reliable and an administration that is accountable to its public”.

Further, according to 1992 report on “Governance and development”, the World Bank defined good governance as “the matter in which power is exercised in the management of a country’s economic and social resources for development”.

In 1994, the Bank sustained the definition, “Governance is epitomized by predictable, open and enlightened policy making (that is, transparent processes); a bureaucracy imbued with a professional ethos; an executive arm of government accountable for its actions; and a strong civil society participating in public affairs; and all behaving under the rule of law”.

According to Organization of Economic cooperation and Development (OECD) governance is defined as “the use of political authority and exercise of control in a society in relation to the management of its resources for social and economic development”.

Thus, Good Governance signifies a participative manner of governing that functions in a responsible, accountable, and transparent manner based on the principles of efficiency, legitimacy, and consensus for the purpose of promoting the rights of individual citizens and the public interest, thus indicating the existence of political will for ensuring the material welfare of society and sustainable development with social justice.

The 8 major characteristics of good governance are it is participatory, consensus-oriented, accountable, transparent, responsive, effective and effective and efficient, equitable and inclusive and follows the rule of law.

Principles of Good Governance by United Nations

1. **Participation:** The involvement of both men and women is the keystone of good governance. Participation could be either direct or through legitimate intermediate institutions. It includes that people should be able to voice their own opinions through legitimate immediate organizations or representative. Participation includes men and women, vulnerable sections of society, backward classes, minorities, etc. It implies the freedom of association and expression

2. **Rule of Law:** It requires fair legal framework should be enforced impartially on human right laws. Impartial enforcement of the laws in the community requires an independent judiciary and police forces.

Without the rule of law, the principle of matsya nyaya will be followed in politics which means the stronger will prevail over the weak.

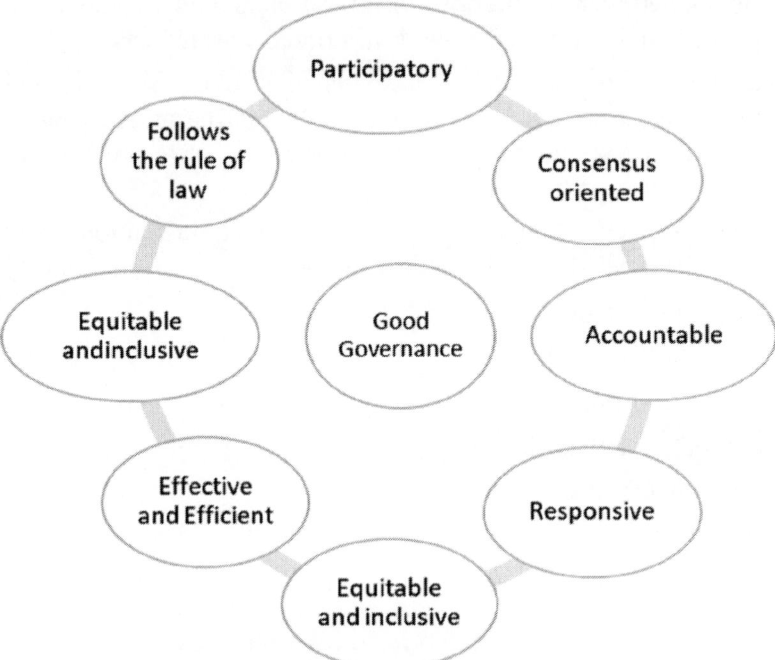

Principles of Good governance

3. **Consensus Oriented:** Consensus oriented decision-making ensures that even if everyone does not achieve what they want to the fullest, a common minimum can be achieved by everyone which will not be detrimental to anyone. It also requires a broad and long-term perspective on what is needed for sustainable human development and how to achieve the goals of such development. It mediates differing to meet the broad consensus on the best interests of a community.
4. **Equity and Inclusiveness:** Equitable society should be ensured under good governance. All the members of the society should feel they have stake in it and do not feel excluded from the mainstream of society. People especially most vulnerable should have opportunities to improve or maintain their well-being.
5. **Effectiveness and Efficiency:** Processes and institutions should be able to produce results that meet the needs of the society with the best use of the resources at their disposal. Resources of the community should be used efficiently to for maximization of output an profit.

6. **Accountability:** Good governance aims towards betterment of people, and this cannot take place without the government being accountable to the people. Government institutions, private sectors, and civil societies should be accountable for public and institutional stakeholders.
7. **Transparency:** There should be transparency in the availability and accessibility of the information to the public and should be understandable and monitored. It also means free media and access of information to them.
8. **Responsiveness:** Good governance requires that institutions and processes try to serve all stakeholders within a reasonable timeframe.

Attributes of Good Governance

1. Rightsizing governmental functions
2. Greater use of information technology and management techniques
3. Delegation, ethics and participation
4. Ensuring accountability
5. Institutional reforms

13

Government and Good Governance

Government

Government is a territorial based body that makes authoritative decisions (for which it has constitutional or legislative authority) that are binding on residents and businesses within its boundaries. It is the executive arm of the state. Government refers to actions carried out within a formal legal setting; governance involves all activities of government along with formal activities even outside a formal governmental setting, which are meant to achieve common goals.

Governance is the process of governing through which decisions are made that are intended to affect societal outcomes, including economic, social, environmental and other important outcomes. It encompasses the direct and indirect roles of formal institutions of local government and government hierarchies, as well as the roles of informal norms, networks, community organizations, and neighborhood associations in pursuing collective actions.

Governance is broader in nature than government. It denotes collective actions of network of multiple actors- state, private sector, civil society etc. Governance denotes the process of decision making and their implication. In governance approach to PA, Civil society, private sector, media, NGOs, and many other.

Government Vs Governance

Comparison point	Government	Governance
Structure	Executive arm of the state	Network of state, public and private sectors, civil society, NGOs, etc.
Role and Function	Agenda setting, policy-making, Implementation	Same-Agenda setting, Policy-making, Implementation
Authority/ Power	Formal/legal authority & power	Both formal and informal authority/ power
Treatment of citizen	To be served, guided, steered	As active participant in decision making and implementation
Role of state	Supreme, solar actor, all authority/power vested in state	Major actor, authority/power decentralized, de-centred in multiple actor

Role of political parties	Very important. The majority party sets the agenda and guide policy formulated and their implementation	Diminished; society as a whole sets agenda, take policy decisions and implement them
Theoretical underpinnings	Representative democracy, Bureaucratic theories, organizational theories	Democratic citizenship, critical theories, public discourse

Good Governance and India

The idea of Good Governance is as old as Indian civilization. in Indian scriptures Good Governance is called *Raj Dharma*, i.e., righteous duty of the king it means those who are involved in governance must adhere to righteousness and do justice to the public. It has inseparable link to social welfare and inclusive development. Absence of good governance has been identified as the root cause of many of the deficiencies in society. It robs the citizenry of their social and economic rights. Good governance signifies basic parameters such as rule of law, participatory decision-making structure, transparency, accountability, responsiveness, equity and inclusiveness. The country's administration has to run on these principles. This necessitates a reorientation in the outlook of the civil services.

When during 1990s World Bank raised the issue of governance, this immediately, became an issue of concern in India. The document of the Ninth Five Year Plan (1997-2002) released in April 1999 included a Chapter on "Implementation, Delivery Mechanism and Institutional Development." In this chapter a review had been done on implementation of five year plans in India with a view to identify weak spots in the formulation and implementation of plan programmes to find solution to the weaknesses. The issue of decentralization in development planning, accountability of the implementing agencies and monitoring and evaluation of programmes were raised.

This was followed by a more specific chapter titled, "Governance and Implementation" in the tenth five year plan (2002-2007). It defines Governance as "the management of all such processes that, in any society, define the environment which permits and enables individuals to raise their capability levels, on one hand, and provide opportunities to realize their potential and enlarge the set of available choices, on the other. These processes, covering the political, social and economic aspects of life impact every level of human enterprise, be it the individual, the household, the village, the region or the national level. It covers the State, civil society and the market, each of which is critical for sustaining human development. The State is responsible for creating a conducive political, legal and economic environment for building individual capabilities and encouraging private initiative. The market is expected to create opportunities for people. Civil society facilitates the mobilization of public opinion and peoples' participation in economic, social and political activities. It further added that "the universally accepted features of good governance are the exercise of legitimate political power; and formulation and implementation of policies and programmes that are equitable, transparent, non-discriminatory, socially sensitive, participatory, and above all accountable to the people at large."

The eleventh five year plan (2007-2012) signifies that the vision of inclusive growth, reducing poverty and bridging the various divides that continue to fragment our society can only be achieved if there is a significant improvement in the quality of governance. There are many different definitions of good governance but it is generally agreed that good governance must be broadly defined to cover all aspects of the interface between individuals and businesses on the one hand and government on the other.

The twelfth five year plan (2012-2017) defines good governance as an essential element of any well-functioning society. It ensures effective use of resources and deliverance of services to citizens and also provides social legitimacy to the system.

Nature of Good Governance in India

The eleventh five year plan (2007-12) highlighted the following features of Good Governance in India:

1. As a democratic country, a central feature of good governance is the constitutionally protected right to elect government at various levels in a fair manner, with effective participation by all sections of the population. This is a basic requirement for the legitimacy of the government and its responsibility to the electorate.
2. The government at all levels must be accountable and transparent. Closely related to accountability is the need to eliminate corruption, which is widely seen as a major deficiency in governance. Transparency is also critical, both to ensure accountability, and also to enable genuine participation.
3. The government must be effective and efficient in delivering social and economic public services, which are its primary responsibilities. This requires constant monitoring and attention to the design of our programmes. Where the responsibility for delivery of key services such as primary education and health is at the local level, this requires

a special attention for ensuring the effectiveness and efficiency of local governments.

4. Governments at lower levels can only function efficiently if they are empowered to do so. This is particularly relevant for the *Panchayati Raj* Institutions (PRIs), which currently suffer from inadequate devolution of funds as well as functionaries to carry out the functions constitutionally assigned to them.
5. An overarching requirement of good governance is that the rule of law must be firmly established. This is relevant not only for relations between the government and individuals, enabling individuals to demand their rights, but also for relations between individuals or businesses. A modern economic society depends upon increasingly complex interactions among private entities and these interactions can be efficiently performed only if legal rights are clear and legal remedies for enforcing these rights are swift.
6. Finally, the entire system must function in a manner which is seen to be fair and inclusive. This is a perceptional issue but it is real nonetheless. Disadvantaged groups, especially the SCs, STs, minorities and others, must feel they have an equal stake and should perceive an adequate flow of benefits to ensure the legitimacy of the State.

14

Attributes of Poor Governance

Poor Governance

Bad governance refers to how decisions are made in government and business. It is opposite of good leadership. Poor governance entails systemic corruption and a lack of openness and accountability, arbitrary policymaking, and the deception of those who are ruled.

Causes of Poor governance

Lack of accounatbility and voice	• Poor governance occurs when governing entities refuse to listen to the voices of those they managed and are not willing to take responsibility for the conduct
Political underdevelopment	• It is caused by state leaders' lack of reliance on their populace. Further, the variance in state functioning is primarily due to wide variance ins tate-society relationship patterns.
Corruption	• Corruption and poor governance often go hand in hand. Presence of crime within a governing body leads to poor governance becasue officials priotise their interests over others.

Attributes of Poor Governance

- Poor management of economy, persisting fiscal imbalances and regional disparities in the pace and level of development across regions and across districts
- Denial of basic needs (food, water and shelter) to a substantial proportion of the population.
- Threat to life and personal security in the face of inadequate state control on law and order

- Marginalisation and exclusion of people on account of social, religious, caste or even gender affiliation.
- Lack of sensitivity, transparency and accountability in many facets of the working of State machinery, particularly those that have an interface with the public.
- Lack of credibility- the gap between the intent and the actions – of some institutions in society;
- Lack of sensitivity, transparency and accountability in many facets of the working of State machinery, particularly those that have an interface with the public
- Delayed justice.
- Existence of a significant number of voiceless poor with little opportunity for participating in governance, despite a visible movement towards decentralized through the Panchayati Raj institutions;
- Deterioration of physical environment, particularly in urban areas.

15

Steps Taken for Good Governance in India

Good governance is crucial for the effective functioning and development of any country, including India. To ensure good governance, several steps have been undertaken in India. Here is an introduction to some of these steps;

1. Strengthening the Democratic Decentralization

The 73rd and 74th Amendments to the Constitution of India are pivotal in strengthening democratic decentralization in the country. These amendments, passed in 1992, provide constitutional recognition and support for local self-governance in rural and urban areas, respectively. The 73rd and 74th Amendments establish Panchayats (rural local bodies) and Municipalities (urban local bodies) as institutions of self-government. They empower these local bodies with the authority to plan and implement economic development programs, social justice initiatives, and the provision of essential services within their jurisdictions.

By enshrining the provisions for local self-governance in the Constitution, the amendments give legitimacy and permanence to the roles and responsibilities of Panchayats and Municipalities. It ensures that democratic decentralization becomes an integral part of India's governance structure. Three-Tier System: The amendments establish a three-tier system of local government, consisting of village/ward-level, intermediate (block/taluk), and district levels for rural areas, and ward-level, ward committees, and the municipality level for urban areas.

The 73rd and 74th Amendments emphasize the devolution of powers and functions to Panchayats and Municipalities. They assign a range of subjects such as agriculture, health, education, water supply, sanitation, and urban planning to the local bodies, enabling them to address the specific needs and priorities of their respective areas. The 73rd and 74th Amendments have played a crucial role in decentralizing power, promoting grassroots democracy, and fostering citizen participation in local governance in India. They have paved the way for inclusive and participatory decision-making processes, bringing government closer to the people and addressing the specific needs and aspirations of different regions and communities.

2. The Right to Information Act

The Right to Information Act (RTI Act) was passed in India on October 12, 2005. It was enacted to ensure transparency and accountability in the functioning of the government and to empower citizens by granting them the right to access information held by public authorities. The primary use of the RTI Act is to enable citizens to obtain information from government departments, ministries, and public institutions. It allows individuals to seek information regarding government policies, decisions, records, budgets, public service delivery, and other relevant matters. This information empowers citizens to make informed decisions, participate in democratic processes, and hold the government accountable for its actions.

The beneficiaries of the RTI Act are the citizens of India. Any individual, irrespective of their age, gender, or occupation, can exercise their right to access information under this Act. It is particularly valuable for marginalized communities, activists, journalists, NGOs, and individuals seeking redressal or clarification on government policies and actions. The RTI Act has brought about significant positive changes in the country. It has increased transparency in governance, curbed corruption, and promoted good governance practices. The Act has empowered citizens to exercise their right to information and has acted as a catalyst for social and economic development. It has fostered greater accountability and responsiveness from public authorities, leading to improved public service delivery and citizen satisfaction. This act has played a crucial role in transforming the relationship between the government and its citizens, making the administration more open, participatory, and accountable. It has empowered individuals to actively engage in decision-making processes, contributing to a more democratic and transparent society.

3. Provision of Right to Work by MGNREGA

The Mahatma Gandhi National Rural Employment Guarantee Act (MGNREGA) was launched in India in 2005. It was previously known as the National Rural Employment Guarantee Act (NREGA) before it was renamed in 2009 to honor Mahatma Gandhi's vision of empowering rural communities. MGNREGA aims to provide social security and livelihood support to rural households by guaranteeing at least 100 days of guaranteed wage employment in a financial year. This program helped in poverty alleviation and focused on creating durable community assets through labor-intensive projects. These projects include construction of roads, water conservation structures, irrigation facilities, and rural infrastructure development. These assets benefit rural communities and contribute to local development. MGNREGA has a specific focus on women's participation and empowerment. It ensures equal wages and opportunities for women, promoting gender equality and empowering women in decision-making processes.

MGNREGA has played a vital role in improving rural livelihoods, reducing poverty, and empowering marginalized communities in India. It has provided employment opportunities, created assets, and enhanced social and economic well-being in rural areas.

4. Right to Education Act

The Right to Education Act, also known as the Right of Children to Free and Compulsory Education (RTE) Act, is a landmark legislation enacted in India in 2009. It guarantees free and compulsory education to all children aged 6 to 14 years, making education a fundamental right for every child. This Act, guarantees free and compulsory education for children aged 6 to 14 years. It ensures access and enrollment without discrimination, sets quality standards for infrastructure and teachers, promotes inclusive teaching practices, and requires private schools to admit students from disadvantaged backgrounds. The Act emphasizes neighborhood schools, provides financial provisions, establishes monitoring mechanisms, and safeguards child rights within the education system. Its implementation aims to increase enrollment, reduce dropouts, bridge educational gaps, promote social equality, and empower children through education.

5. Provision of Effective Rural Healthcare

The National Rural Health Mission (NRHM) is a program launched in 2005 to provide accessible healthcare in rural areas. It strengthens healthcare infrastructure, trains healthcare professionals, and ensures the availability of essential drugs. NRHM focuses on maternal and child health, providing antenatal care, safe delivery services, and immunization. Community participation is encouraged through Village Health and Sanitation Committees. Robust health information systems aid in data management and decision-making. Public-private partnerships are promoted for better healthcare delivery. Quality assurance measures are implemented, including infection control and monitoring. NRHM aims to bridge the rural-urban healthcare gap and improve overall health in rural communities.

6. Right to Food Act

The National Food Security Act (NFSA), enacted in 2013, aims to provide food security to vulnerable populations in India. It strengthens the Targeted Public

Distribution System (TPDS) to ensure subsidized food grains reach eligible beneficiaries. Approximately 75% of the rural and 50% of the urban population are covered under the Act. It emphasizes the provision of nutritious meals to pregnant women, lactating mothers, and children through existing programs. The Act promotes women's empowerment by designating them as the head of households for receiving food grains. Grievance redressal mechanisms are established, and a transparent and accountable system is implemented. Food security allowances act as safeguards for non-compliance. Overall, the NFSA strives to reduce hunger, improve nutrition, and enhance food security among vulnerable populations.

7. Launch of Government Web Portal

The Governance Knowledge Centre (GKC) was launched in 2005 by the Department of Administrative Reforms and Public Grievances (DARPG), Government of India. It is a web-based platform that aims to improve governance in India by providing information, resources, and advocacy on good governance practices. The GKC covers various topics such as public policy, administration, finance, transparency, and citizen participation. It offers case studies, best practices, tools, templates, and training modules to assist government officials, civil society organizations, and citizens. The GKC not only provides valuable information but also engages in outreach activities to raise awareness and promote the adoption of good governance practices. It is a vital resource for enhancing the effectiveness and accountability of government in India.

8. Administrative Reforms

Administrative reforms and public grievances are vital components of good governance. Administrative reforms focus on improving the efficiency and effectiveness of government processes, enhancing service delivery, and adopting citizen-centric approaches. Public grievances address the concerns and complaints raised by citizens, ensuring their voices are heard and their issues are resolved. The Department of Administrative Reforms and Public Grievances (DARPG) in India spearheads these efforts, coordinating administrative reforms and facilitating the timely resolution of grievances. These initiatives aim to foster transparency, accountability, citizen participation, and trust, ultimately contributing to the overall development and welfare of society.

9. Direct Benefit Transfer Scheme

The Direct Benefit Transfer (DBT) scheme, launched in India in January 2013, is a government initiative that brings several benefits to welfare programs. By delivering welfare benefits and subsidies directly to the bank accounts of beneficiaries, the DBT scheme ensures transparency, efficiency, and accountability. It eliminates intermediaries, reducing leakages and corruption in the system. With the DBT scheme, ghost beneficiaries are identified and removed, ensuring that the benefits reach the intended recipients. The scheme promotes financial inclusion by providing beneficiaries with direct access to their entitlements. It also streamlines the delivery process, making it more convenient for beneficiaries and reducing administrative burdens. Overall, the DBT scheme has revolutionized the distribution of welfare benefits, enhancing the effectiveness and impact of social welfare programs in India.

10. Launch of e-Governance

The National e-Governance Plan (NeGP) was launched in India in 2006 to transform the delivery of government services through the use of information and communication technologies (ICTs). Implemented in phases, the NeGP aims to make services more accessible, efficient, and transparent. It has made significant achievements, including providing over 1000 government services online, processing over 1 billion online transactions, registering over 100 million citizens for online services, and training over 100,000 government employees on e-governance. The NeGP has been recognized globally, winning awards for its effectiveness. It has made government services more citizen-centric and laid the foundation for an efficient and transparent governance system in India.

11. Digital India

The Digital India mission, launched in July 2015, aims to transform India into a digitally empowered society and knowledge economy. It focuses on digital infrastructure, services, and empowerment. By providing high-speed internet connectivity and digital platforms for government services, the mission enhances access, transparency, and efficiency. It promotes digital literacy, enabling citizens to participate in the digital economy. The mission fosters innovation, entrepreneurship, and the growth of the digital industry. Overall, the Digital India mission drives digital transformation, improves service delivery, and bridges the digital divide in India.

12. GST (Goods and Services Tax)

The implementation of the Goods and Services Tax in July 2017 aimed to simplify India's complex tax structure and create a unified and transparent tax system. GST has streamlined taxation processes, reduced tax evasion, and improved the ease of doing business.

13. Swachh Bharat Abhiyan (Clean India Mission)

Launched in 2014, the Swachh Bharat Abhiyan aims to achieve universal sanitation coverage and make India open-defecation free. This cleanliness campaign emphasizes the importance of cleanliness and hygiene and focuses on constructing toilets, promoting waste management, and creating awareness about sanitation practices.

14. National Programme for Civil Services Capacity Building (Mission Karmayogi)

Mission Karmayogi, known as the National Programme for Civil Services Capacity Building (NPCSCB), is an administrative reform initiative introduced in India. It was officially announced by the Union Cabinet on September 2, 2020. The primary objective of this mission is to establish a strong foundation for enhancing the skills and capabilities of government employees in India, thereby promoting good governance. Mission Karmayogi is a program aimed at improving how the government manages its employees. It has the following features like, the proposed changes in employee job assignments aim to prioritize qualifications and skills rather than strict rules. Training will be provided in the workplace, complementing external training. A unified training system will be established, ensuring all employees have access to the same resources. The FRACs method will define roles, activities, and skills for government jobs, while also shaping training content. Civil servants will enhance their competences through self-directed and mandatory learning programs. A collaborative learning ecosystem will be created among central ministries, departments, and affiliated organizations, supported by annual financial subscriptions. Partnerships with content creators, including training institutions, universities, start-ups, and experts, will contribute to a comprehensive capacity-building strategy.

Bibliography

"Building a Strong Democracy: Rights, Institutions, and Good Governance in India" by Siddharth Gupta Year of Publication: 2022 Publisher: Lexicon Books

"Constitutional Democracy: Rights, Institutions, and Governance" by Rajesh Mishra Year of Publication: 2023 Publisher: Liberty Press

"Decentralized Democracy: Unraveling Local Governance and Empowerment" by Priya Verma Year of Publication: 2021 Publisher: Nimbus Publishers

"Democracy in Action: Exploring Rights, Institutions, and Effective Governance" by Deepa Sharma Year of Publication: 2023 Publisher: Prodigy Publications

"Democracy's Triumph: Exploring Rights, Institutions, and Good Governance" by Arjun Singhania Year of Publication: 2020 Publisher: Harmony House

"Local Governance in India: Empowering Democracy at Grassroots" by Neha Gupta Year of Publication: 2022 Publisher: Citrus Publications

"Strengthening Democracy: Challenges, Innovations, and Good Governance" by Anjali Singh Year of Publication: 2021 Publisher: Insight Books

"The Evolution of Democracy: Principles, Challenges, and Governance in India" by Ravi Kapoor Year of Publication: 2023 Publisher: Enlighten Books

"Unveiling Democracy: Principles, Challenges, and Governance" by Maya Sharma Year of Publication: 2021 Publisher: Alpha Books

Democratic Visions: Understanding the Essence of Democracy" by Alok Kumar Year of Publication: 2022 Publisher: Horizon Publications

Development and Democracy in India by Shailendra D. Dharma, 2002. Lynne Rienner, Boulder.

The Constitution of India, by P. M. Bakshi. 2017. Universal Law Publishing. Edn.: 14th

Index